SETH-SMITH

Lord Paramount of the turf.

*Lord Paramount
of the Turf*

The 1844 Derby, won by the fraudulent Running Rein.
Engraving by J. F. Herring, Snr. (By courtesy of Fores Ltd., London)

Lord Paramount
of the Turf

LORD GEORGE BENTINCK 1802–1848

✳

MICHAEL SETH-SMITH

FABER AND FABER

3 Queen Square

London

First published in 1971
by Faber and Faber Limited
Printed in Great Britain
by Ebenezer Baylis and Son Limited
The Trinity Press, Worcester, and London
All rights reserved

ISBN 0 571 092047

Author's Note

Although the French Revolution and the ascendancy of Napoleon Bonaparte resulted in war between England and France, the turmoil had little affect on Racing England. Villainy and fraud were rampant, and only Newmarket controlled by the Jockey Club. Fifty years later the greatest Derby fraud was history, and Victorian England was enjoying the sport of horseracing, which had been given a new image of honesty and morality. The life of Lord George Bentinck covers this period, for he was born in 1802 four months after the signing of the Peace of Amiens and died in September 1848. During my researches into his racing career and the era in which he lived, many people generously gave me their help. I am especially grateful to the Duke of Portland for his kindness in allowing me access to the Portland Papers in the Manuscript Department of the University of Nottingham, and for permission to quote letters from them. At the University Mrs. M. A. Welch, Keeper of the Manuscripts, and Mr. Alan Cameron took immense trouble on my behalf. The Duke of Richmond permitted me to reproduce letters from the Goodwood Papers in the County Archives at Chichester, and I was given much help by Miss Taylor, assistant to Mr. Ralph Hubbard at Goodwood. I also wish to thank the Trustees of the Duke of Newcastle for permission to use an extract from the Newcastle Diaries, Lord Derby, Lord Mostyn, Mr. David Weatherby, Mr. Eric Birley, Major J. Fairfax Blakeborough, Mr. Matthew Murphy, Dr. A. D. Thomson and the Director of the Bowes Museum. Finally I would like to thank my wife Mary for all her encouragement.

Illustrations

Acknowledgement is made to the National Portrait Gallery for plates 4, 5, 6, 10, 12, 13; for plates 8, 9, 11, 14, 15 from Goodwood House, by courtesy of the Trustees; to Arthur Ackermann & Son for plates 16, 17, 18, 19, 20, 21, 22, 23; to the *Illustrated London News* for plates 24, 25, 26, 27, 28, 29; and to the Honourable Society of the Inner Temple for plate 7.

I

The rising sun gave promise of a fine September day as Mr.
Philip Falkner, Coroner of Newark, set out for Welbeck Abbey,
home of the Duke of Portland. The news of the sudden death of
Lord George Bentinck had been brought to him the previous
morning, and with it a personal request from the aged Duke
that an inquest on his son be held as soon as possible. Distorted
versions of how Lord George had died had already reached the
local villages, and as Mr. Falkner rode towards Welbeck he saw
that notices announcing the death had been pasted in the windows
of those shops which sold newspapers. He arrived at the Abbey
to learn from servants, stunned and shocked by the tragedy, that
arrangements for the inquest had been made. He learned also
that Lady Charlotte Bentinck was the only one of the Duke's
sons and daughters present to console her widowed father, for
the Marquis of Titchfield was in London, Lord Henry Bentinck
was shooting in Scotland, and Lady Howard de Walden was in
Brussels.

At eleven o'clock the jury, consisting of local gentleman
farmers, were ushered into one of the rooms of the Abbey and
were sworn in by Mr. Falkner. Outside the sun blazed down
upon the estate workers as they laboured to bring in the last of
the harvest; but within the temporary courtroom there was a
gloom born of sadness as the jurors moved forward to see the
body of Lord George Bentinck. To them he had been a distinguished and admired aristocrat whose actions had made him a
legendary figure throughout the length and breadth of England.
They were mystified that he had died so unexpectedly, for even

9

though he had spent the entire year in arduous and prolonged wrangle and debate in the House of Commons, he had seemed in cheerful mood at Doncaster races the previous week. Two years had elapsed since his famous 'sky blue white cap' racing silks had been seen on a racecourse, but after the Derby winner Surplice, whom he had bred and sold as a yearling, had won the St. Leger he had remarked that he hoped to return to the 'Sport of Kings'.

The first witness called by Mr. Falkner was William Perks, a footman who had been in the service of the Duke of Portland for seven years. He stated that on Thursday morning Lord George Bentinck had breakfasted with his father, his sister and Sir William Simons before retiring to his room. During the morning he had answered letters from the Duke of Richmond and Lord Enfield, and had written a seven-page letter to his political colleague Benjamin Disraeli, whose reputation as the author of *Coningsby* and *Sibyl* had already been surpassed by his ability as a Parliamentarian. He remained in his room at lunch time, and was not seen again until he left Welbeck Abbey shortly after four o'clock, to walk three miles to Thoresby Park where he intended to stay with Lord Manvers.

A Welbeck stableman, Richard Lenthall, told the jury that he had driven Lord George Bentinck's valet across to Thoresby in the late afternoon, and that they had seen his lordship walking along the footpath at the edge of the deer park. It was a path along which the Duke of Portland frequently took his afternoon walk, but on the day in question he did not leave the Abbey. Lenthall added that he had been called out of bed late at night and asked if he had any news of Lord George, who had not arrived at Thoresby, where Lord Manvers had delayed dinner for more than an hour. When there was no sign of his guest he had sent the valet back to Welbeck in a gig. Lanterns were fetched and a search made of the paths along which Lord George would have walked. It was a brilliant moonlit night and, even without the lanterns, there would have been little difficulty in discovering his cold and lifeless body, which was close to the gate leading to the water meadow.

He was lying face downwards, one of his arms under his body, his walking-stick partially underneath him, but firmly grasped in his hand, and his hat a yard or so before him. A little blood had flowed from his nose, and there was blood on the side of his head. Two other estate workers, Richard Evans and his son, told the jury that as they returned from work in the early evening they had seen a man who appeared to be reading, for his head was downcast, standing by the water meadow gate. They were some two hundred yards away and did not recognize him. After the Coroner had confirmed that Lord George's body had been carried back to Welbeck Abbey on a break, the inquest continued with medical evidence being given by two doctors. Dr. John Shirley Hayes stated that he had arrived at the Abbey at two o'clock in the morning, shortly before the dead man had been brought back by the servants. After the clothes had been removed, he had made an examination of the body and noted that there was a great deal of contusion about the left eye—such contusion as would be produced by a fall. The bridge of the nose was also slightly injured, but there was no mark of any violence. The left side of Lord George's tongue appeared to have been injured by his teeth, and there was a considerable amount of blood under the skin on his right side. In his pockets were his betting book, a gold pencil case, twelve gold sovereigns, twenty-eight shillings and sixpence in silver and his pocket book containing a cheque for one hundred pounds, two five pound notes and some other papers. He was wearing a gold watch and chain and two gold rings.

Mr. Hayes explained to the jury that after he had completed his examination, he was joined by Doctor William Squires Ward, who had known Lord George for many years and had been his regular medical attendant when he had been at Welbeck Abbey. Together they opened Lord George's head and body. There was little food in his stomach and no morbid appearance beyond the congestion which prevailed over his whole system. There was a good deal of emphysema of the lungs and old adhesions from former disease, especially in the dead man's right lung. His heart, which was large and muscular and covered with fat, was empty of blood and bore the appearance of irregular contractions. His brain was healthy, with a little congestion.

It was almost two o'clock when the Coroner began to read the depositions of the witnesses. He mentioned that it was a pity that Gardner, Lord George's valet, was not present—but he had been sent to London; he also commented that he did not think that the jury would have any difficulty in accepting the evidence of the doctors. None of Lord George's money or valuables had been stolen, and there were no marks of injury which might have suggested that he had been attacked and robbed. Within moments of Mr. Falkner concluding his remarks the jury returned their verdict that 'His Lordship had died by the visitation of God, to wit, of a spasm of the heart', thus ending the rumours and gossip which had been spreading throughout the neighbourhood, that murder or suicide were possible causes of his death.

However, Lord George Bentinck's death is veiled in mystery, despite the verdict of the jury. No comment was made at the inquest regarding the fact that a man with Lord George's heart condition should not have attempted a walk of several miles. No comment was made by Doctor Ward that Lord George had not eaten since breakfast, and yet a few days after the inquest the doctor told the Curate of Badsworth—a village in the neighbourhood of Welbeck—that in his opinion Lord George should not have died, as when his pockets were emptied there were notes and coins of every description in them. If sixpence of the money had been expended on a mutton chop and eaten before he started out for Thoresby, he would have remained alive.

The possibility that Lord George was murdered does not warrant consideration and suicide is equally unlikely, notwithstanding local village rumours which prevailed until after the inquest. Admittedly it is conceivable that Lord George could have taken poison without the two surgeons discovering traces in his body, but if he had done so, it is probable that there would have been some clue from the contents of his pockets. The state of his heart and excessive over-work might have caused acute depression, but the possibility of suicide seems so remote that it must be discarded.

A theory which seems less improbable is that his death was brought on by shock, either immediate or delayed. Remorse can remain perpetually and many of his actions throughout his racing career could not, by any stretch of imagination, be described as wholly honourable. Blackmail was not unknown in the middle of the nineteenth century, and if he had been accosted at Doncaster races during St. Leger week and threatened with some form of exposure, this could have indirectly caused his death by bringing on a heart attack.

Another possibility is that he could have been accosted during his walk to Thoresby and given news that so shocked him that in his over-wrought state his heart was unable to withstand the strain. In a letter written less than a year previously he had admitted 'I worked upon my spirit in 1846 & 1847, but I have learnt now that I have shaken my constitution to the foundation, and I seriously doubt my being able to work on much longer'.

The day after Lord George Bentinck died the Duke of Newcastle rode over to Welbeck Abbey to inquire after the eighty-year-old Duke of Portland. In his diary, he wrote:

'I found the Duke had been told of the event at about 12 o'clock and had received the sad news with more calm than they expected, but that he was, as the servants described it, dreadfully "cut up" as well he might be by such a bereavement.

'Thus has his country lost the most valuable public man in it. The only honest, fearless and unconquerable politician in public life whose career has been like a meteor, full of fire and transcendent brightness and like fire, purifying all it touched.

'While he lived, political treachery and rascality were impossible. He would bare them to the bone, and with a proven ability that no sophistry could withstand and no mean artifice could cover. Such a man will not be found again, few such men have been seen before him: he was a patriot in public and a real friend in private life . . . '

Two days later the Duke of Newcastle referred again in his diary to Bentinck's death:

'I hear today that nothing has occurred in the post-mortem examination of Lord George which can guide them to any conclusion as to the cause of his deeply lamented death. His excessive and incessant labours were a sufficient cause—they would have killed any other man in much less time . . . '

Lord Henry Bentinck arrived from Scotland two days after

the inquest, but was so overwrought by his brother's death, that Doctor Ward returned to the Abbey to look after him. The Duke, however had recovered sufficiently from his initial grief to leave his room and, despite the pleas of his family, insisted on visiting the water meadow where his son's body had been found.

For the remainder of the week the coffin containing Lord George Bentinck's body rested in the library at Welbeck. Three sculptors took casts for busts before the coffin, covered with crimson velvet, was taken on a special train to London for burial in the Portland family vault in Marylebone Old Church. On the morning of the funeral it rained heavily and the streets were almost deserted as the hearse, drawn by six horses, left Harcourt House in Cavendish Square. Ships anchored in the Thames flew their flags at half mast, and eulogies were written in Lord George's honour. Lord John Manners wrote to his father, the Duke of Rutland: ' . . . this awful catastrophe which has deprived us of the most true, warm hearted of friends, and the Country of the purest, most self-denying least selfish of patriots.' His cousin Charles Greville, with whom he had quarrelled bitterly admitted in his diary that he was a 'very remarkable man' who as leader of the Protectionist party was, for a brief moment, a potential Prime Minister. Disraeli described him as an 'English Worthy' and 'the Lord Paramount of the British Turf'. He was born in an era when the Turf offered blacklegs, tricksters and nobblers ample opportunity to enrich themselves, and only Newmarket was under the control of the Jockey Club, of which he became the most influential member, responsible for many of the innovations which redeemed the tarnished reputation of English racing. He maintained the largest racing establishment in the land, was the scourge of those whose skullduggery made honest men despise the Turf, and at times took the law into his own hands to defeat their villainy. His energy and initiative in Parliament and the Law Courts did much to unravel the involved and antiquated Gaming Laws of England. His intervention into the fraud of the 1844 Derby which resulted in the ruin of the perpetrators, brought him public acclaim and a testimonial from his fellow members of the Jockey Club. When he died Victorian England was enjoying a sport which had been given a new image of honesty and morality.

No wonder he was a hero to so many who did not appreciate that he was also proud, arrogant, unrelenting, self-opinionated and vindictive in his hatred for those who thwarted him. If he was defeated he sought revenge, if he conquered he counted his gains, as Greville wrote in his Diary, 'as a general counts his prisoners after a battle.' His code of morality and honour was inconsistent, for he would have no qualms in acting in a manner which would bring forth tirades of abuse if he found others behaving in similar fashion. He was accused by Greville of 'thundering away against poor low rogues for the villainies they have committed whilst he has been doing things which high-minded men like his father would think nearly if not quite as discreditable and reprehensible'. His high-minded father was one of the richest men in the country, his grandfather a Prime Minister of England, and yet Lord George Bentinck died a lonely bachelor who had not made a will.

2

Lord George Bentinck's ancestor, William Bentinck, born in 1649, had been a page of honour in the household of William III, Prince of Orange and, as a young man, made several confidential missions to England on behalf of his Royal Master. Throughout the momentous events following the landing of William III at Torbay, William Bentinck was constantly at the Prince's side. He was amply rewarded for his loyal service, and a few days before the coronation was created Baron Cirencester, Viscount Woodstock and Earl of Portland. Until William III's death he was his most trusted diplomatic agent, and in 1698 was appointed Ambassador to France. He died in November 1709, and was succeeded by Henry Bentinck his only surviving son by his first wife, Anne Villiers.

In 1716 King George I bestowed the dukedom of Portland upon Henry Bentinck in recognition of his father's achievements. Four years later the newly created Duke lost much of his inherited wealth when the disastrous 'South Sea Bubble' burst, and in his efforts to recoup his fortune he accepted the Governorship of Jamaica. The family wealth remained in jeopardy until his son William married Lady Margaret Cavendish Holles Harley who, on the death of her mother in 1755, inherited the Welbeck Abbey estate in Nottinghamshire.

Margaret's father, Edward Harley, second Earl of Oxford, approved of the match and in a letter to Swift had referred to Bentinck as 'a man free from the prevailing qualification of the present set of young people of quality, such as gaming, sharping, pilfering and lying. . . . '

William, the second Duke of Portland died seven years later,

1. 4th Duke of Portland, father of Lord George Bentinck

2. Crucifix, ridden by J. B. Day, winning the 1840 Oaks

3. Surplice, winner of the 1848 Derby and St. Leger, and bred by Lord George Bentinck

and for the next twenty-three years the new Duke quarrelled with his mother over their financial affairs. It was agreed that she should live at Bulstrode, the Buckinghamshire estate owned by the Bentinck family, whilst he lived at Welbeck Abbey. Twice Prime Minister of England he was constantly beset by lack of money in his domestic life, and from a financial point-of-view his mother's death in 1785 was opportune. His political career left him insufficient time to devote to the management of his estates, and he seemed to prefer Bulstrode to Welbeck. In August 1795 his eldest son married Henrietta, daughter of Major General John Scott of Balcomie, County Fife, and it was decided that they should make Welbeck Abbey their home. The General was a renowned gambler, but unlike so many of his contemporaries, who thought nothing of risking an inheritance or an estate upon the turn of a card, he both made a fortune and retained it. It is reputed that he won more than £100,000 at Whites Club, principally by his skill at whist and his refusal to befuddle his brain with food and wine. He was content to dine off boiled chicken, toast and water and come to the gaming table clear headed. His fortune was divided between his three daughters, the 'witty' Miss Scott who married Hon. George Canning, the 'pretty' Miss Scott who married the Earl of Moray, and the 'rich' Miss Scott who married the Marquis of Titchfield, later fourth Duke of Portland, who had been elected Member of Parliament for Petersfield in 1790 and the following year Knight of the Shire for Buckinghamshire. For five successive Parliamentary elections he held this seat unopposed, but although he was encouraged by his brother-in-law George Canning, his heart was not in the cut and thrust of political life, but rather in the loving care and management of his estates. When he inherited the Dukedom in 1809 he also acquired debts of more than half a million pounds. Many of these debts were settled by the sale of Bulstrode, and part of the family property in Cumberland. Wise stewardship of the remainder of his inheritance, aided by the era of prosperity which England was entering, completed the recovery of the Portland fortunes. The value of his property in Marylebone soared, and before the middle of the nineteenth century his income exceeded £100,000 a year.

The Duke was interested in the breeding of racehorses, although he only maintained a few mares at his Welbeck stud. His policy was to engage several of the leading jockeys to come to Welbeck after the St. Leger meeting at Doncaster in September to try out his two year olds the best of whom were sent to be trained by Richard Prince at Newmarket. One of the Duke's idiosyncracies was his belief that none of his horses should be allowed on a racecourse until they were indifferent to all noise. In his efforts to reach this state of affairs he insisted that they were marched past a drum and fife band, were shouted at, and had pistols discharged at close quarters until they remained tractable and calm no matter how much hullabaloo was occurring.

The Duke, who was elected a member of the Jockey Club in 1810, had his greatest success on the Turf when Tiresias won the 1819 Derby beating Mr. Crockford's Sultan by a head. He hardly ever missed a day's racing at Newmarket where he had a wagon constructed which he used as a moveable grandstand. On the wagon was a powerful telescope through which he watched the races, audibly announcing how the various runners were progressing. He usually dressed in a blue coat with gilt Jockey Club buttons, leather breeches and top boots. The noise and bustle of Epsom were anathema to him, but at Newmarket he found a peace which greatly appealed. He never gambled, and wished that his beloved Newmarket could be rid of the blacklegs who brought it into disrepute.

The Duke's nine children were brought up at a time when England was in the throes of the Napoleonic Wars. The defeat of the French at Waterloo was a time of national rejoicing, in which children shared, even in the vastness of Welbeck Abbey. The Duke was reluctant to send his children to school, and was content that they were under the tutelage of the Rev. D. H. Parry, the chaplain at Welbeck. His eldest son was eventually sent to Christ Church, Oxford, where he showed promise as a classical scholar, although he was accused of being indolent and lacking in any form of passion. Elected as Member of Parliament for King's Lynn in 1822, he died two years later and was succeeded as Marquis of Titchfield by his brother John, who as a young man found more pleasure in fox hunting than in any other pastime. He too, was accused of being listless and indolent, and spent much of his life travelling on the continent, satisfied to leave politics and Society to others. For a short space of time he was in the army, but even life as a cavalry officer offered little appeal. He was persuaded in 1824 to succeed his brother as member for King's Lynn—but within two years had resigned in favour of his younger brother Lord George Bentinck.

There was nothing untoward in the childhood of Lord George, born on 27th February 1802. He was sent neither to Eton nor Christ Church, and spent the first seventeen years of his life in the peace and solitude of Welbeck. He learnt to ride and to fish and shoot, but academically his education was not of a high standard. He was brought up in an atmosphere of leisure, but not culture, surrounded by servants who were at his beck and call; and he missed the harsh benefits which public schools provided. His father did not seem to have special plans for his future, and the army was considered a suitable career for a third son who showed no desire to enter the Church. Consequently as a young man of eighteen he was commissioned as a cornet in the 9th Royal Lancers. Nicknamed 'George the Second' after an incident when he had acted as second to one of his brother officers, he appeared to be lacking in humour, and unappreciative of the practical jokes which were a favourite pastime of his fellows. On one occasion he returned from a dinner party to find his bedroom at Chatham Barracks filled with stray dogs, chickens and a goat—and took the prank with singular bad grace, much to the amusement of the instigators. It was his misfortune that there was no war in which his leadership and courage would have been at a premium. As a peace-time soldier he was cussed, offensive and inclined to imagine that the fact that his father was a duke placed him above criticism.

Matters came to a head when Captain Ker, a well meaning and popular officer, took exception to the manner in which he was carrying out his regimental duties. The Captain's displeasure took the form of a letter in which he enumerated a list of special duties which Lord George should carry out as punishment for his behaviour, which was supposedly bad for regimental morale. On receipt of Captain Ker's letter, Lord George promptly sent it to his commanding officer Lt. Colonel Morland, with a request that there should be an inquiry into his conduct as he denied every allegation.

When the Court of Inquiry was held at Romford Barracks on 10th February 1821 these allegations were divided under the headings: 1. Inattention to duty, 2. Contemptuous, insubordinate and disrespectful behaviour. Captain Ker failed to prove his case, the Court found in favour of Cornet Lord George Bentinck on both counts and Captain Ker was compelled to apologize. There the affair should have ended, particularly as Lord George Bentinck left the regiment to take up the duties of Private Secretary to his uncle by marriage, the Hon. George Canning. Canning had been appointed Governor General of India and it was intended that Lord George should travel with him as his Military Secretary. These plans were altered, owing to the suicide of Lord Castlereagh, and his luggage, already aboard the frigate *Jupiter*, was hastily disembarked. Canning became Foreign Secretary and Leader of the House of Commons and thought it expedient, much to the pleasure of the Duke of Portland, to allow his young impetuous nephew to continue to serve on his staff.

Whilst Canning and Lord George were in Paris, Captain Ker, still misguidedly smarting under the indignity of being supposedly ridiculed by a junior officer, followed Bentinck to France. The sympathy anyone may have had for him up to that moment vanished, for he was carrying his bitter recriminations to extremes. Bentinck, who regarded the entire affair as tedious, thought that the way to pacify Ker was to agree to any demands he made, and did not demur for an instant when it was dramatically proposed that they fight a duel at seven o'clock in the morning in the Bois de Bologne.

With the thoughtlessness of youth it never crossed Lord George's mind that his uncle, Canning, might be appalled at the possible outcome of this meeting—and would interfere. In fact Canning, far more wise than his brash young relation credited, knew from the outset how the affair was progressing. He was in communication with Captain Ker's Commanding Officer, and he knew exactly when Ker arrived in Paris and that he was staying at the Prince Regent Hotel. So, too, did the Paris police. Almost as soon as the antagonists, their seconds and a surgeon arrived in the Bois de Bologne the police surrounded them and insisted that the affair should not be renewed in France. The explanation as to why the duel was not stopped earlier is given in a letter from Canning to Lord George's father:

'I was perhaps chiefly determined to it by the reflection that nothing but an actual meeting could entirely save George from misconstruction. In fact nothing could be more clear and courageous than his whole conduct. During the ten days or thereabouts that the matter was pending, nobody could have inferred from his manner or conversation that he had anything unusual upon his mind . . . .'

Captain Ker persuaded himself that the only reason that the French police interfered was because they had been 'tipped off' by Lord George, who was too much of a coward to stand his ground. This far-fetched notion was broached in a letter that Ker sent to Lieutenant Huntley—one of his brother officers. Huntley, inexcusably, read the letter aloud in the Officers' Mess, thus heaping coals upon the fire. The unfortunate affair was completely out of proportion, and authority intervened in the personage of H.R.H. Frederick, Duke of York, the Commander-in-Chief, who ordered a further inquiry into the conduct of the participants. The findings of the new inquiry, endorsed by the Commander-in-Chief gave Captain Ker two choices, a trial before a General Court Martial or the liquidation of his commission. Neither alternative appealed, but as the choice of evils he elected to retire on half-pay. He died of cholera in Paris shortly afterwards. Thus ended the quarrel, which had begun by Lord George's reluctance to obey the commands of a senior officer to whom he had taken a dislike. Throughout the incident there were those who attempted to discredit Lord George by insisting that, from lack of bravery, he would never fight a duel. Years later they were to be proved wrong.

By the time Lord George reached his majority in 1823 he was a man of more than six feet in height who dressed elegantly, without bowing to fashion or dandyism. He did not make friends easily, and was bored by the incessant merry-go-round and inconsequential life of London Society. The question which vexed him most was how should he spend his life. He had already seen enough of the army to realize his ambitions did not lie in that direction, and the same applied to a political career. Canning was his political hero, and he had enjoyed his association with his uncle by marriage, for at times he had felt that he was at the hub of Cabinet affairs, but he disliked the devious paths which Parliamentarians followed to achieve recognition and posts of high office. He needed an interest more direct, more stimulating, where success would depend on his own initiative. It was unlikely that he would ever become Duke of Portland, and so the management and improvement of the Welbeck estate would be a task for his elder brothers. In consequence, like so many other men of wealth, ability and leisure, he turned to the Turf.

He rode for the first time in public when he competed in a race at the Goodwood meeting of 1824. He was staying at Cowdray Park and his host, Mr. Poyntz who had married a sister of Viscount Montague, invited him to ride a mare named Olive in the Cocked Hat Stakes, a race in which riders wearing cocked hats were allowed six pounds. The invitation, though unexpected, was accepted. One of the ladies' maids was given some silk with which to make a racing-jacket, whilst a cocked hat was procured from the local hatter. Lord George's style of riding left much to be desired, and was reminiscent of the hunting field, but he won the final heat, beating Captain Frederick Berkeley on the fancied Goodwood runner Swindon. The excitement of this success made him more anxious than ever to devote his life to the Turf despite the disapproval of his father.

This disapproval was understandable and in some respects justified for the Turf, in the early part of the nineteenth century, was the meeting ground of the gambling, pleasure-seeking section of the aristocracy, and also of those to whom villainy was second nature. The racecourses were frequented by thimble riggers, tricksters and gangs of ruffians who terrorized spectators and fought pitched battles amongst themselves. At one Doncaster meeting a troop of Dragoons were brought from Sheffield to assist the local Justices of the Peace to round up and convict more than one hundred thieves, pickpockets and confidence tricksters. At Cambridge Daniel Dawson was publicly hanged for poisoning Newmarket racehorses, and the frauds and swindles perpetrated by bookmakers such as 'Crutch' Robinson were everyday events over which the Jockey Club had little control. Horses were doped, pricked on shoeing, 'pulled' and watered before starting. At some country meetings the jockeys rode at incorrect weights and used whips loaded with quicksilver when on the weighing scales.

The Prince Regent had given up racing at Newmarket after his disagreement with the Jockey Club in 1791, and outwardly took little interest in racing, except in the horses owned by his profligate brother Frederick, Duke of York. In London William Crockford was on the threshold of harvesting a fortune, and the nightly exploits at the card table of Lord Chesterfield, King Allen, Ball Hughes and many others became the exaggerated gossip of Society, as they discussed the gains and losses of these Corinthians. It was into this dissolute world of gambling and racing, where gentlemanly bearing and calm demeanour were considered by Society to be more important than the loss of an inheritance, that young Lord George Bentinck plunged.

3

The Duke of Portland, worried at the amount of time that Lord George spent on the racecourse, made strenuous efforts to turn his son's energy and initiative into other channels. He gave him Muirkirk, an estate in Ayrshire, and was delighted when he succeeded his elder brother as Member for King's Lynn—a constituency he represented for the rest of his life. Lord George was not enthusiastic about becoming a Member of Parliament, but he wished to please his father, and also believed that he would enjoy meeting in the House of Commons those with whom he had become friendly when he had acted as Canning's Private Secretary. Another reason why he wished to please his father was that the Duke had just completed generous financial provision for all his children. His share consisted of one sixth of a settlement of £40,000, a life interest in two sums invested in 3½% Stock, one amount being for £20,000 and the other £30,000, and a life interest in the North Lynn estate, which yielded £1,500 a year, out of which £500 was paid to the Marquis of Titchfield, and £300 to Lord Henry Bentinck. These financial provisions meant that his resources were ample, although his capital was not sufficient to allow him to spend extravagantly in excess of his income. At the 1826 Doncaster St. Leger meeting, he rashly backed the favourite Belzoni as though defeat was impossible, and faced ruin when the horse failed to win. No exact figure of his loss is known, although an amount of £30,000 has been estimated. Sensibly he admitted his debts to his family. His mother and his sister helped him to settle his wagers, and so too did his father, to whom he wrote at the end of September:

24

'The steps which you propose to take to relieve me from my present embarrassment are liberal beyond anything I could possibly have contemplated, and of course proportionally agreeable to me and I am thankful in the same degree for them, and I am also to you for leaving it in my power to continue those of my former amusements which carry with them no risk of fortune.' 'No risk of fortune' implied an intention to stop gambling, but Lord George did not do so. If an excuse was needed to account for his constant appetite for the excitement and exhilaration which betting in large amounts provided, it was the example of his grandfather the gambling General Scott. If an influence was required it was provided by his cousin Charles Greville.

Charles Greville was nearly eight years older than Lord George. His mother, Lady Charlotte Bentinck, was the Duke of Portland's sister who had married the Right Honourable Charles Greville—a grandson of the 5th Earl of Warwick. As a boy Greville spent much of his time at Welbeck where he became a special favourite of the Duke. While at Eton, where he impressed his tutors by his scholarly style of writing, he went to Epsom to see the Duke of Grafton's Pope win the 1809 Derby, and became fascinated by the atmosphere of the racecourse. On leaving Eton he went to Christ Church before being appointed Secretary to the Earl of Bathurst, Secretary of State for War and the Colonies. Greville's finances were based upon the fact that at the age of seven he was appointed Secretary of the Island of Jamaica, in reversion on the death of Mr. Charles Wyndham, and at the age of ten given an even more exacting post—that of Clerk Extraordinary of the Privy Council, without salary, but with right of succession as an ordinary clerk on the death of Lord Chetwynd. These astonishing sinecures would ultimately bring in an income of £5,000 a year, but until the death of Lord Chetwynd in 1821 Greville was in debt. In a letter to Lord George's father, written in March 1821, Greville admitted to debts of over £8,000 which included losing bets as to when Lord Chetwynd and Mr. Wyndham would die. Not included in these amounts was a sum of £700 which the Duke had lent him to settle losses incurred over the previous year's Derby. All these outstanding debts were paid, largely due to loans and guarantees provided by the Duke of

Portland who warned his nephew of the follies of gambling, in similar manner as he had warned his own sons.

At the same time as Greville was receiving financial help and advice from Lord George's father, he was accepting the Duke of York's request that he managed his racehorses. For years Greville had been a frequent visitor to Oatlands at Weybridge where the Duke held open house to his gambling friends. Whist and Macoa were played every evening, and after one particular occasion the twenty-five-year-old Greville wrote in his diary:

'Some may be unfitted by nature or taste for Society, and for such gaming may have a powerful attraction. The mind is excited. at the gaming table all men are equal. no superiority of birth, accomplishments, or ability avail here. great noblemen, orators, merchants, jockeys, statesmen and idlers are thrown together in levelling confusion.'

In 1822 the Duke of York's Moses won the Derby, and Greville who was more impressed than other spectators by Moses' previous victory at Newmarket won a substantial amount in bets.

It is understandable that events such as this made Greville seem a dashing hero to his young cousin, Lord George Bentinck. Greville, described by a contemporary as 'high bred, with a square and sturdy figure, and a mouth tense and exquisitely chiselled', was the friend of everyone of social or political importance. His younger brother was Private Secretary to the Duke of Wellington which added further family prestige.

An unforseen event, the death of the Duke of York in February 1827, was a cause of the cousins joining forces, for although King George IV decided to resurrect his racing interests and bought some of his late brother's horses, there was no question of Greville being appointed his racing manager. Greville was in a predicament. What was he to do? The proposal that attracted him most was that he should become the partner of his wealthy cousin, to whom racing had become a ruling passion. George Canning's death in August 1827 cut away another steadying influence on the headstrong Bentinck, who persuaded his brothers to guarantee him a credit of £300,000 at Drummond's Bank as an additional source of capital for his racing activities, should his losses be prodigious. He was instinctively honourable

26

where the settlement of his own debts were concerned and expected others to be equally high principled, even though his principles did not prevent him from attempting to befool those with whom he bet, by disguising the merit and ability of his horses. It disillusioned him when he realized that the racing world was full of charlatans to whom the word 'honour' was meaningless and the evasion of the payment of their debts a dire necessity. He would never tolerate any proposal to pay losing wagers other than in full settlement, and carried his morality even to the extent of proclaiming in Crockford's that a certain member should not order an expensive dinner until he settled his outstanding gambling debts. His most serious problem was how to hoodwink his father as to the scale of his interest in racing. In consequence some of the first horses that he owned in 1825 and 1826 ran in the name of Mr. Samuel King and his son-in-law Mr. John Bowe, who kept the Turf Tavern at Doncaster. When he bought more horses he began to use the names of his friends, and many of the horses entered by the Duke of Richmond, Lord Lichfield, and Lord Orford were in reality his property. It was an unsatisfactory arrangement and made the suggested alliance with Charles Greville seem heaven sent. Here was a man whom he admired, of his own flesh and blood, willing to help him exert his influence over the sport of horseracing, increase his fortune, find glorious success in winning every important race in the Calendar, and into the bargain rid the Turf of the scoundrels and blackguards whom he despised.

The racing partnership between Lord George and Charles Greville did not meet with great success until the autumn of 1834 when their filly Preserve was acknowledged to be the best two-year-old filly in training. She had been bred by Charles Greville and was sired by Emilius, the 1823 Derby winner. Her racecourse debut was impressive when she won the Clearwell Stakes at the Second Newmarket October meeting, notwithstanding the efforts of some of the jockeys deliberately to delay the start of the race. Almost one hour was wasted in false starts, and during this time a thunderstorm followed by torrential rain made the horses both fractious and frightened. A fortnight later Preserve won the Criterion Stakes at the Houghton meeting, and forty-eight hours later a match with odds of 5–2 laid on her.

The 1835 flat-racing season opened auspiciously for Greville and Bentinck when Preserve, ridden by Nat Flatman won the 1,000 Guineas at Newmarket by three lengths. There were only two races that afternoon as four stake races due to be run on the same day were inadvertently not advertised until half-past five on the previous evening instead of appearing in the morning list. The conditions of these races stated that entries closed at 6.0 p.m.—and as between 5.30 and 6.0 p.m. no trainer or owner looked at the notice board, there were no entries.

On all known form Preserve was a certainty for The Oaks and Lord George backed her accordingly. Greville was less interested in betting than his cousin, and objected to the subterfuges employed to extend the price of horses that Lord George wished to back at Tattersalls. Before The Oaks it was announced that Preserve was suffering from influenza, and her nostrils were painted with a mixture of starch, flour and water to resemble mucus in an effort to deceive the touts who watched her at exercise, and thus to lengthen the odds. The effort was to no avail as she started favourite at 7–4 on. Rumour claimed that Greville gave different instructions to Preserve's jockey in the paddock to those previously agreed with Lord George, and this caused a rift between them. Whilst the fillies were parading in front of the Grandstand one wiseacre shouted 'Preserve is all gammon—Queen of Trumps is the mare' and his prediction proved correct for Queen of Trumps won easily with Preserve second.

The rift between the cousins widened as a result of Preserve's subsequent races at Goodwood. She won the opening race of the meeting and the following afternoon was started for the Goodwood Stakes. Greville also ran another horse in the race—Dacre, a four year old by Bizarre,—who was one of the outsiders. Lord George was convinced that Preserve would win and played up his gains from successful bets made on the Tuesday afternoon. Dacre made the early running, until a furlong from the winning post he was joined by Lord Chesterfield's Glaucus with Preserve close up and obviously full of running. As Preserve challenged Dacre leant on her and forced her to swerve, allowing Glaucus to win by a length. Lord George was indignant and believed that the incident was a deliberate attempt to prevent him from winning.

His relationship with Greville gradually deteriorated into bitter animosity from this moment. Years later, at the time of Bentinck's death, Greville recalled the incident in his diary and wrote of it:

'Till then not an unkind word had ever passed between us, nor had a single cloud darkened our habitual intercourse; but on this occasion I opposed and thwarted him, and his resentment broke out against me with a vehemence and ferocity that perfectly astounded me, and displayed in perfection the domineering insolence of his character. I knew he was out of humour, but had no idea that he meant to quarrel with me, and thought his serenity would speedily return. I wrote to him as usual, and to my astonishment received one of his most elaborate epistles, couched in terms so savage and so virulently abusive, imputing to me conduct the most selfish and dishonourable, that I knew not on reading it whether I stood on my head or my heels.'

Despite the Goodwood fiasco, Bentinck was convinced that Preserve was beaten entirely on merit in The Oaks and consequently retrieved all his losses by backing Queen of Trumps when she won the St. Leger at Doncaster. In his efforts to safeguard his substantial wagers by ensuring Queen of Trumps' peak fitness, he persuaded her owner to change the scene of her final gallops from the sandy soil of Holywell in North Wales to the softer downs of Hednesford, where there was less likelihood of her breaking down. There were only eleven starters for the St. Leger, partly due to the ground having been hard all summer, and the consequential crippling of many horses, and partly due to the fact that, of the original 67 horses entered, nineteen had come from Scott's Malton stables, and only two of these ran. Nevertheless on St. Leger day, in the presence of the Duchess of Kent and her daughter, Princess Victoria, Queen of Trumps won impressively, and her defeated rivals included not only Preserve, but also Mündig the Derby winner. Three days after her St. Leger victory, Queen of Trumps was brought out again to compete against two moderate opponents. She started at 10–1 on and was beaten, owing to a bulldog rushing on to the course and bringing her to her knees just as she was making her challenge. Such is the fate of 'racing certainties'.

Within days of the St. Leger, news came from Ireland of an

incident concerning the age of a filly which was the harbinger of similar cases of greater significance in future years. The difficulty of determining a horse's age had been a problem for centuries, and in the past ten years there had been at least one fraud of substitution perpetrated at York races, whilst in 1826 there was some doubt as to the correct age of the Earl of Egremont's Derby winner Lapdog. In 1833 Mr. Fores of Piccadilly published a pocket map of the age of horses as shown by the teeth, and claimed that the nine coloured maps would prove a useful manual for purchasers of horses. The following year the Jockey Club decided that 'horses shall be considered at Newmarket as taking their ages from 1st. January' and this step cleared away much confusion. It did not, however, prevent the unscrupulous from attempting to perpetrate fraud by running three year olds in races exclusively for two year olds—races in which they would have a distinct advantage. Anyone who could successfully deceive the racing world as to the correct age of his horses stood to win a fortune by gambling.

The news from Ireland was that the Earl of Miltown claimed that Mr. Ruthven's Caroline filly, which had run at The Curragh in a race for two year olds, was in reality a three year old. Ruthven insisted that his filly was a two year old by Sir Hercules out of Wegenkorb, while Lord Miltown insisted that the filly was none other than Beccassine, once owned by Sir Mark Wood and sold by him to George Payne, from whom Squire Osbaldeston bought her for £250 on behalf of Ruthven. Lord Miltown, to prove his case, requested that the filly be produced for examination. This request was refused by Ruthven, who was a member of the Dublin Turf Club. Osbaldeston, to vindicate his part in the affair, wrote to Bell's *Sporting Life* claiming that, after he had bought Beccassine for Ruthven, he had received a letter from Ruthven stating that the mare had been sold to a gentleman named Jones in Manchester who shipped her and several other thoroughbreds to America. Lord Miltown called a veterinary surgeon who stated that he had examined the mouth of the Caroline filly at the recent race meeting at Naas. In his opinion she had the mouth of an old three year old, with six teeth full shot out. He mentioned that the stableboy looking after her had told him that the filly had won races in England, and innocently added that Mr. Ruthven had been extraordinarily generous to him! Lord Miltown also produced a letter from Charles Greville who wrote that Beccassine was a chesnut, slight, bloodlike, with white down her face, stilty of right forelegs, frequently in season, and light rather than dark in colour. Greville who had gone to much trouble to acquire an accurate description of Beccassine suggested that the filly be sent over to Newmarket for further examination, and added that she had a black spot upon one of her quarters, one white heel behind and some white above the girthing place besides white hairs on many parts of her body. Letters concerning Beccassine were also received from Mr. Tattersall, George Payne and Lord George Bentinck. At this moment Ruthven resigned from the Dublin Turf Club—an action which was not interpreted as that of an innocent man. At a meeting of the Irish Stewards in December it was agreed that a substitution tantamount to fraud had been made. In their efforts to hush up the affair the Stewards issued a report which concluded '. . . we feel imperatively called upon to remark that in consequence of Mr. Ruthven's withdrawal of his name from the Turf Club, it does not become a part of our painful duty to recommend to the Club any further proceedings in this matter.'

The proof of Ruthven's guilt and the total lack of any civil prosecution, illustrated the power and authority of the Dublin Turf Club merely to ban those whom they considered guilty of misdemeanours. The fact that there were no criminal proceedings must have encouraged others to believe that, even if they abused the code laid down by the Turf authorities, this would not make them liable to criminal prosecution.

It was this attitude which so exasperated and infuriated Lord George Bentinck, that he deemed it justifiable to take the law into his own hands when dealing with malefactors who were antagonistic to the authority of the Jockey Club.

4

A week after the St. Leger, a race-meeting was held at Heaton Park, the Lancashire home of the Earl of Wilton. Even by the unethical standards of the day this annual event was an astonishing affair.

It was traditional that each year the handicapper was the guest of the Earl. In return for hospitality he was expected to weight favourably any horses either owned by those who were in the Earl's house party, or horses trained by John Scott. Scott was allowed to train his horses during race-week on the private gallops at Heaton Park, but all other trainers were compelled to work on Manchester Racecourse, notoriously one of the worst maintained tracks in England. Eventually several outraged owners rebelled against these conditions and refused to allow their horses to run at Heaton Park races, which became a mockery and a farce. Squire Osbaldeston, however, decided to attempt to defeat both the handicapper and the Earl of Wilton's house guests, who included Lord George Bentinck, still flushed with success from the St. Leger meeting.

The exploits of Osbaldeston, born in 1786, as a shot, as a Master of Hounds and as a cricketer, had made him the hero of sporting England, and his match against time at Newmarket on Saturday 5th November 1831, when he had wagered a thousand guineas that he would ride 200 miles in less than 10 hours, enhanced his reputation. In fact he completed the ride in the phenomenal time of 8 hours 42 minutes, even though it rained heavily throughout the first three hours.

Osbaldeston judged that the best way to bamboozle the

5. Lord George Bentinck, bust by Campbell

4. Lord George Bentinck, by Lane

7. Baron Alderson

6. Sir Alexander Cockburn

handicapper for the Heaton Park races was to enter a horse who was an unknown quantity. It was generally agreed that the ability of horses bred in Ireland was inferior to their English rivals and in consequence the handicappers were inclined to treat them with scorn.

Osbaldeston determined to take advantage of this, and bought, for 400 guineas, a four-year-old colt named Rush, who had won several Queen's Plates in Ireland. In the light of the notorious affair of the Caroline filly, it is significant that Osbaldeston bought Rush from Mr. Ruthven. The purchase was made the week before the St. Leger, and Osbaldeston, anxious to find out Rush's ability, rode him in a trial gallop over the St. Leger course at 6 o'clock on the morning of the race. Although he was uncertain as to how good or bad a horse Rush might be, the Squire was determined that the touts should be none the wiser, and hoped that, by holding the trial at dawn, he would find them still in bed! At the end of the first three quarters of a mile Rush was pulling over his galloping companion and then began to forge ahead when, to his consternation, the Squire saw a group of touts standing near the winning post. He promptly pulled up Rush and allowed the other horse to catch up and pass him. The watchers were deceived, and Osbaldeston dismounted, happy in the knowledge that Rush had proved, to his satisfaction, that he had sufficient ability to win at Heaton Park.

During the next three days Rush was walked from Doncaster to Manchester. On the first day of the Heaton Park meeting Osbaldeston rode two of his own horses which were unplaced, thus implying that his stable was out of form. The meeting had got off to a successful start as the winning owner and jockey of the first race was Lord Wilton who to the delight of his guests, also rode the winner of the first race on the second day. Later in the afternoon Rush competed in the Manchester Stakes and finished fourth to the four-year-old filly Lady de Gros, ridden by Lord Wilton. On the final day of the meeting the principal event was held, the Gold Cup, which was given by the town of Manchester. There had originally been 39 subscribers, but 28 of them paid 5 sovereigns forfeit. Amongst the starters were Rush and Lady de Gros. The previous day, when Lady de Gros had beaten Rush, she had carried 11 stone 9 pounds and Rush 10 stone 9 pounds. In the Gold Cup, (in reality two large oval waiters to stand on a side-board), the filly was set to carry 12 stone 2 pounds and Rush 10 stone 2 pounds, a difference of a stone in the colt's favour compared with the first time they met.

On the eve of the race there was hectic betting amongst Lord Wilton's guests at Heaton Park, and George Payne astutely took 10–1 to win several thousands about Rush's chances. Lord George Bentinck was accepting bets on the race, and laid Rush so heavily that before the afternoon of the race, he became favourite at 2–1. Amongst those who backed Rush with him was Osbaldeston. On the way to the starting post, the Squire took the precaution of going up to the judge and demanded that the unfortunate man took a good look at his colours, at the same time warning him that he would win and would not excuse any mistake on his part in favour of Lord Wilton. Osbaldeston, even though a man of only 5 foot in stature, was not to be trifled with, and the judge, who the previous afternoon had awarded a race to Lord Wilton which he had palpably lost, realized that here was an instance where he had to act both honestly and impartially.

Once the race started, Rush delayed his challenge until inside the final 100 yards and won in a canter from Lady de Gros. Considering that the filly had raced and won on the first day of the meeting, and again on the second day, she must have been exhausted and, added to this, she was giving Rush 2 stone. Nevertheless Lord Wilton and Lord George Bentinck were indignant and considered Osbaldeston a cheat, especially as Rush was brought out again and won a Free Handicap later in the day, which they thought added insult to financial injury.

Jealousy is an odious characteristic, but it is understandable that Bentinck bitterly resented the manner in which the Squire had befooled him. The actual wager was of little significance, a paltry £400, but the snub was there for all the Heaton Park guests to see. Whatever feelings he may have harboured against Osbaldeston, however much he begrudged the Squire's conduct, he should have settled the wager without argument, particularly as his moral code insisted on settlement from others.

Normally debts were settled at Tattersalls every Monday, and it was assumed that Lord George's debt to the Squire would be paid on the Monday following the Heaton Park meeting. In fact Bentinck decided not to pay and some time elapsed before Osbaldeston went up to him and requested settlement. 'Do you mean to say, Sir', Bentinck replied 'that you dare to ask me for the money for that robbery—for it was a robbery and you know it'. It was both madness and folly to make such a remark to one of the most celebrated shots in England, for there was no doubt that he would promptly send Lord George a challenge. Osbaldeston was a man of fifty, sixteen years older than Lord George, but the outcome of such a duel was a foregone conclusion—Lord George would be dead. Osbaldeston went to George Payne, his lifelong friend, and requested that he acted as his second.

George Payne was two years younger than Lord George Bentinck and ought to have been an immensely rich man, for on coming of age he had inherited Sulby Abbey in Northampton-shire, and an income of £30,000 a year. His father had been killed in a duel by the brother of a girl he had seduced, when young George was a boy of only six. At five o'clock one morning he had left the card table with an apology that he had an important engagement to fulfil. He drove to Wimbledon Common where the girl's brother was awaiting him. Mr. Payne was a crack shot, but told his second that whatever happened he would not return his adversary's fire. He kept his word, but was himself shot in the groin and died that afternoon in the Red Lion at Putney.

Seven years later young George Payne's uncle's horse, Azor, won the 1817 Derby and gave him the 'flavour' of the Turf. His career at Christ Church, Oxford, left much to be desired scholasti-cally, and he departed from the University long before any question of studying for a degree was muted. He is reputed to have lost over £30,000 when Jerry was beaten in the 1824 St. Leger, and this was only the beginning of a reckless life of gambling, both on the racecourse and at the card table, which made inroads into his assets. He was unlucky in that he never owned a brilliant horse, but he took his losses philosophically and was a much admired, popular and respected man in the London clubs, on the Turf and in his home county of Northamp-tonshire. He hunted the Pytchley in extravagant style for three seasons, and for many years was the racing confederate of Charles Greville, after Greville and Bentinck had parted company. By nature a cheerful man who loved the dissolute life that he and his many friends led, he was seldom downcast by misfortunes. One evening when he had been losing at Crockford's, a member happened to ask Crockford whether he preferred Champagne Mousseux or Champagne Sillery—to which he replied 'I like George Payne better than either'.

Payne had won a considerable sum over Rush's victory, and had hunted and shot with the Squire for years. Nevertheless he refused to act as his second and the Squire went to his London club, ironically the Portland, to find a substitute. Colonel Dacre agreed to act and then changed his mind. Ultimately a Mr. Humphrey agreed to act, whilst Lord George persuaded Colonel George Anson to act on his behalf. All Lord George's friends were aghast at the certain outcome of the duel, and beseeched him to apologize. Their time was wasted, and undaunted and obstinate he made plans to fight the Squire at 6 o'clock in the morning at Wormwood Scrubs. The previous afternoon his friends, in desperation brought him a letter which they had composed, in the hope that he would sign it and allow them to send it to the Squire. Typically he considered it tantamount to an apology and tore it up.

Even at this stage, George Payne persisted in his efforts to prevent the duel. After midnight he saw Osbaldeston at the Portland Club and delivered his final ultimatum, an ultimatum which in his heart Osbaldeston knew to be justified, and which they argued about for almost two hours. It was that if he killed Lord George no man would ever speak to him again, not because of Bentinck's death, but because they all believed that what had been said about Rush cheating was true. To add further warning, Payne ended by telling the Squire that he too, even though he had won money over the race, was convinced that Rush's victory was virtually a fraud. Payne's efforts were to no avail, and the next morning the two antagonists met as arranged. Lord George was dressed from head to foot in black, and walked up and down impatiently whilst awaiting the Squire's arrival. That the affair did not end in disaster was due not only to George

Payne, but also to the wisdom and advice of Colonel Anson, who pointed out to the antagonists that if either killed the other and the affair came before the Law it would be a clear case of murder, and would be based upon the evidence that he would most certainly give. In his efforts to confuse the duelists Anson instructed them to fire immediately he exclaimed 'three'. The Squire and Bentinck then moved 12 paces apart and awaited Anson's command. The word 'one' was followed by a long pause. Expecting a similar pause after 'two' they were both surprised by three' being shouted in the same breath. The inexperienced Bentinck excitedly fired in the air, and Osbaldeston, deliberately aiming high, merely shot through Bentinck's hat, when he would have had no difficulty in killing him.

For several years the two men never acknowledged each other's existence, but eventually when Lord George wished to become a member of the Bibury Club, the Squire made it clear that he had no intention of 'black-balling' him. Returning to Harcourt House, his father's London home, Lord George wrote to the Duke on 14th April:

'My dear Father,

George Anson has kindly undertaken to write you an account of my affair with Osbaldeston. I do not expect you will do otherwise than condemn the folly and indiscretion in the first instance in telling the man the truth to his face;—but I trust you will at the same time think I was at least right in morality as well as in honour when once I had uttered a charge, which in my conscience I believe to be just, to adhere to it and firmly refuse to retract or to qualify it.

I hope there is no man who would be more ready or anxious to make fullest reparation and the most ample and humble apology, than I should be, where any honest man could pretend I had wronged or done injustice in the slightest degree to another;—but where I was well assured I had done neither wrong nor injustice but spoken out the truth, and nothing but the truth, I should have been ashamed of myself if I could have been contented to purchase personal security by sacrificing the truth and denying the truth for any personal consideration.

The difficulty O. found in getting any man to accompany him,

37

and eventually declaring himself satisfied with one shot without so much as the whisper of any apology or retraction from me are incontestible proofs of the justice of my accusation.

With respect to George Anson, I can never forget the real kindness, ability and earnestness with which he managed my part in the transaction, not fearing to identify himself with every charge I had made, whilst he left no stone unturned to induce Mr. Humphrey to throw up his commission.

I go to Newmarket on Saturday, and shall be very impatient till I hear from you that you think I was morally speaking right, however you may condemn my folly and rashness in the first instance. . . . '

Years later George Anson was to be Commander-in-Chief in India at the time of the outbreak of the Indian Mutiny. News of the Sepoy Rising was brought to him by telegram as he was about to entertain guests for dinner, and the telegram remained unopened for several hours as he considered it would have been bad manners to open it before the departure of his guests. Within days he was dead, the stress and strain of his military duties in the heat and dust of a rebellious India being too much for him.

5

A month after his duel with Osbaldeston, Bentinck saw Lord
Jersey's colt Bay Middleton win the Derby. Classic victories were
not unknown to Lord Jersey, for since 1824 when his filly Cobweb won the 1,000 Guineas, he had won the 2,000 Guineas with
Riddlesworth in 1831 and then in consecutive years with Glencoe,
Ibrahim and Bay Middleton, and the Derby with Middleton in
1825 and Mameluke in 1827. Lord Jersey never ran his horses as
two year olds, but even so Bay Middleton went to the post for
the 2,000 Guineas with a great reputation, for he had won the
Riddlesworth Stakes at the Craven meeting with consummate
ease, beating Destiny, who subsequently won the 1,000 Guineas.
Bay Middleton's sire was Crockford's Sultan, second in the
1819 Derby to the Duke of Portland's Tiresias; his dam
Cobweb.

In the 2,000 Guineas Bay Middleton's chief rival was Elis who,
although running in the colours of Lord Lichfield, brother-in-law
of George Anson, was owned by Bentinck. Elis had won several
valuable races as a two year old, including four races at Newmarket and the Molecomb Stakes at Goodwood. Lord George
backed Elis heavily for the 2,000 Guineas but, although he ran
creditably, Bay Middleton beat him by a neck. Elis was not
entered for the Derby, and Lord George, believing that Bay
Middleton could not be defeated, wagered with the utmost
confidence, refusing to be put off by the rumours that Bay
Middleton not only had a 'leg', but also an unmanageable temper.
As the runners for the Derby were parading a sporting baronet
asked Lord Jersey his opinion of Bay Middleton, to which the

owner replied 'I beg to refer you to Bland and Greatrex, as they know more about the horse than I do'. Bland and Greatrex were bookmakers!

The Derby result vindicated Lord George's judgement for Bay Middleton won impressively. Many of the aristocrats present at Epsom heard the Hon. Berkley Craven groan 'Jersey wins' as Bay Middleton passed the winning-post and were shocked and saddened when they learned that he returned to London and in the evening shot himself, as he was unable to settle his debts. Greville wrote in his diary:

'It is the first instance of a man of rank and station in society making such an exit. He had originally a large landed estate, strictly entailed, got into difficulties, was obliged to go abroad, compromised with his creditors, and returned, fell into fresh difficulties, involved himself inextricably in betting, and went on with a determination to shoot himself if his speculations failed, and so he did. He was very popular, had been extremely handsome in his youth, and was a fellow of infinite pleasantry and good-humour.'

Amongst those of Craven's friends who saw the Derby were Captain Rous and his bride, married but four months. Craven's death was largely responsible for initiating Rous' life-long dislike of gambling and all its disastrous ramifications.

Bay Middleton enhanced his fame by winning at Royal Ascot, but during the summer Elis had also added to his laurels, and the germ of an idea, ingenious, daring and revolutionary seeded itself in Lord George's mind. It contained so many elements which appealed to his nature that his excitement became boundless, for if successful, his plan would cause consternation to the gambling fraternity whom he so actively disliked.

The crux of the scheme lay in his conviction that Elis was the second best three year old in the kingdom and that Bay Middleton would not run in the St. Leger. Therefore Elis, who after his defeat by Bay Middleton in the 2,000 Guineas, had been sent to be trained by Kent at Goodwood and had won at both Goodwood and Lewes, was prepared for the Doncaster classic and Lord George ordered his commission agents to start backing him for the St. Leger.

In the year 1836 there was only one method of horse transportation, and that was on foot. Most Newmarket horses were sent to the Epsom area a month before the Derby meeting and stabled at Headley, Mickleham, Leatherhead and Ashtead. The tough mare Cyprian, trained by John Scott at Malton, was walked 500 miles on her month-long journey to and from Epsom, where she won the 1836 Oaks, and on her return to Yorkshire was taken immediately to Newcastle to win the Northumberland Plate.

The dangers of the travel, leg weariness, the change of stables and of corn, air and water, all added to the chances of defeat, and scant consideration was given to southern trained horses who travelled north for important races. It was accepted by the racing fraternity, therefore, that if a racehorse was known to be in a certain place on a particular day it was impossible for him to be taken to another in less than a specified time. The bookmakers knew that Elis was at Goodwood.

However, the word 'impossible' was not in the vocabulary of Lord George Bentinck, who remembered that in 1816 springs had been fitted to a bullock caravan which conveyed Mr. Territt's horse, Sovereign, at the rate of 40 miles a day, from Worcestershire to Newmarket for the 2,000 Guineas. Inspired by this innovation, Lord George decided to build a van suitable to take Elis to Doncaster in record time.

Mr. Herring, the Long Acre coachbuilder, was commissioned to construct a van capable of holding two horses, although he was not let into the secret as to why the van was needed. The inside of the box was padded, and the horses stood upon a hard stuffed mattress, so that their knees should not be broken if they fell. Cumbersome though it appeared the van, drawn by six post horses, only took three days to travel from Goodwood to Doncaster. Wide-eyed country folk gazed in amazement as the weird vehicle careered past them, and in the evenings crowds gathered around the van as it rested outside the hostelry surrounded by other carriages. On the road the drivers of phaetons, mail-carts, curricles and gigs pulled up in astonishment and wonder as the van thundered past.

On Sunday evening prior to the St. Leger a halt was made at

Lichfield racecourse. The journey from Lichfield to Doncaster took less than a day, but news of Elis' arrival had already reached the bookmakers, who were flabbergasted as they calculated their losses, should he win the St. Leger. Two factors nearly saved them financially. The first was that, a fortnight before the race, Lord George heard rumours that someone, unknown to him, was steadily backing Elis and that, in consequence, his price was shortening. With typical arrogance, but equally with wisdom, he announced that unless he was given £12,000– £1,000 forthwith, he would scratch Elis from the race. It was tacitly understood that those who had been responsible for backing Elis had their horses trained by the Days at Danebury. The second factor was that the Scotts from Malton thought that their colt Scroggins was unbeatable, and gambled on him accordingly. In the St. Leger Elis, ridden by J. Day, took up the running some three furlongs from home and ran out a two lengths winner, much to Lord George's jubilation.

In the autumn Elis and Bay Middleton met again in the Grand Duke Michael Stakes at Newmarket, and once more Elis was beaten, although Lord George expected this result, for he realized that Bay Middleton was the better horse. Consequently he asked Lord Jersey if he would sell Bay Middleton. The price was agreed at £4,000, a huge sum even for a Derby winner in those days. Bentinck had a regard bordering on an obsession for Bay Middleton, and would have paid even more than £4,000 if he had been compelled to do so, particularly as he hoped to win the 1837 Ascot Gold Cup with him.

Whether or not Lord Jersey knew of Bay Middleton's infirmity is open to question, but shortly after Lord George bought him, Bay Middleton's leg gave way and he never raced again. He had a very high action when galloping slowly and constantly struck the inside of his off knee with his near fore. After he broke down he was sent to Lord George's stud at Doncaster where Ascot, second in the 1835 Derby to Mündig also stood. To Lord George's chagrin Bay Middleton proved a failure at stud for more than ten years, and although he served forty or more well-bred mares every year, most of his offspring were useless. Lord George explained his purchase of Bay Middleton in a letter to his father,

'My dear Father,

I have given Lord Jersey £4,000 for Bay Middleton as a stallion. It seems a large sum upon the first blush of the matter but I think it will turn out a profitable speculation. I have made a table of the average life of thoroughbred stallions, calculated upon the lives of 209 stallions, whose ages at their death are recorded in the Obituary of the Stud Book and I find that the Average Life of a stallion is 20 years + 29 days. This being so, as a mercantile transaction I have a right to calculate upon any horse living that number of years.

This being the foundation of my speculation I think I have a fair right to assume that Bay Middleton will be at the least as popular a stallion as Priam until his stock appear—Priam for 3 years had his subscription full at 30 sovs. a mare & 30 mares— which would produce me £2,700, leaving me after deducting 5% interest upon my capital £1,900 out of pocket. Should Bay Middleton's stock come out & run well there would be little doubt of my continuing to derive the same annual income from him in this country—but supposing him not to prove a good stallion I should probably have the means of ascertaining what was generally thought of his stock, and there would be little doubt of my being able—before his stock actually appeared—of selling him to the Americans for £3,000 or more which would leave me a very handsome profit upon my speculation. I have bought him with the stipulation that he is not to go out of the country without Lord Jersey's consent but that with an understanding at the same time that he will give me that consent should there be reason to believe at the expiration of 3 years that his stock is likely to prove a failure.

My own opinion is that he can scarcely fail to be a good stallion, because first I believe him to be the best horse ever bred in this country & secondly for generations back there is no bad blood, no moderate blood even, on the side either of the dam or sire.

I do not mean to allow him to cover this season for 2 reasons— first because beginning to cover so late in the season he would probably only get refuse mares & young mares hot out of training

43

which might probably be the means of ruining his reputation as a stallion the first year his stock came out & 2nd because I hold an opinion that it is a bad thing for a horse to cover before he gets to his full strength & vigour.'

The 1837 racing season began promisingly for Lord George. He had great hopes for Bay Middleton at stud, and his filly Chapeau d'Espagne won the 1,000 Guineas. But he was disturbed by the advice which his cousin Charles Greville had given him concerning the Duchess of Richmond, and which Greville mentioned for all the world to know after Lord George's death:

'. . . He fell desperately in love, and he addicted himself with extraordinary vivacity to the Turf. At this time and for a great many years we were most intimate friends, and I was the depositary of his most secret thought and feelings. This passion, the only one he ever felt for any woman, betrayed him into great imprudence of manner and behaviour, so much so, that I ventured to put him on his guard. I cannot now say when this occurred, it is so long ago, but I well recollect that as I was leaving Goodwood after the races I took him aside, told him it was not possible to be blind to his sentiments, that he was exposing himself and her likewise; that all eyes were on him, all tongues ready to talk, and that it behoved him to be more guarded and reserved for her sake as well as his own. He made no reply, and I departed. I think I repeated the same thing to him in a letter; but whether I did or no, I received from him a very long one in which he confessed his sentiments without disguise, went at great length into his own case, declared his inability to sacrifice feelings which made the whole interest of his existence, but affirmed with the utmost solemnity that he had no reason to believe his feelings were reciprocated by her, and that not only did he not aspire to success, but that if it were in his power to obtain it (which he knew it was not), he would not purchase his own gratification at the expense of her honour and happiness.'

Caroline, Duchess of Richmond, was the eldest daughter of the dashing Marquis of Anglesey who had lost a leg at the battle of Waterloo. Her mother was Lady Caroline Villiers whose brother the Earl of Jersey sold Bay Middleton to Lord George. There seems little justification for Greville's claim that Lord

44

George was enamoured of the Duchess of Richmond, and no other contemporary report substantiates it.

At the end of the Napoleonic Wars her husband the Duke, returned to Goodwood, but the chest wound he received at the battle of Orthez still caused his medical advisers much anxiety, and on their advice he gave up hunting and turned his attention to the Turf, although it was not until 1823 that he became interested in the sport on anything more than a humble scale. This was partly due to the settlement of debts incurred at the gaming table by his mother, which necessitated financial economy in the running of the Goodwood estate for a considerable period. His interest in racing was fostered by Viscount Dunwich (later the Earl of Stradbroke, elder brother of Captain Rous) who recommended that John Kent, who was training at Newmarket, should come to Goodwood as his private trainer.

One of the first horses that the Duke owned was Dandizette who won several races in his colours of 'yellow, red cap'. At the 1824 Goodwood meeting Dandizette was first past the post, but was not placed either first or second by the judge who was so busy looking at the other runners that he missed seeing her. The judge was none other than Charles Greville! Three years later the Duke's Link Boy won the Goodwood Cup and Gulnare The Oaks. Gulnare was sired by Smolensko, Sir Charles Bunbury's 1813 Derby winner, out of Medora who had won The Oaks in 1814. These triumphs made the Duke branch out further, and at the dispersal sale of the Duke of York's stud he bought Moses, the 1822 Derby winner, in addition to brood mares from Lord Durham. The gallops at Goodwood were so much better than those anywhere else in England, with the possible exception of Newmarket, Danebury, Middleham and Malton, that many of the Duke's racing friends begged to be allowed to have their horses trained at Goodwood. Colonel Peel, Sir James Graham, the Earl of Uxbridge (his brother-in-law) and Charles Greville all sent horses to his stables, until there were nearly 40 horses in training under Kent's supervision. The hospitality and kindness of the Duke was proverbial and his guests found an enjoyment at Goodwood that few other places in England could offer.

In the autumn of 1837 Lord George saw Mango, out of the

same mare as Preserve, win the St. Leger in the colours of Charles Greville, on the same day that the Duke of Richmond paid him £2,000 for seventeen of his yearlings. To add to his satisfaction his two-year-old Grey Momus, bred by Sir Tatton Sykes, had proved one of the best colts of the year, winning three of his six races. The following year Lord George openly raced his horses in his own name and colours, and Grey Momus, trained at Danebury, began his three-year-old career by winning the 2,000 Guineas. Lord Suffield's Bamboo was third, and baffled his Newmarket connections, who thought him to be in the nature of a certainty. So disgusted was Lord Suffield, who blamed his jockey for incompetent riding, that a match was made between Grey Momus and Bamboo for £1,000 a side at the same weights. The race was run the subsequent Friday and Grey Momus won again. Although the match was for £1,000 it was given out that it was for only £300 as it was thought that Lord George's father would strongly object if he learnt the true sum involved.

As a result of his 2,000 Guineas victory, Grey Momus started favourite for the Derby but much to Lord George's disappointment, was beaten one length and three lengths by Sir Gilbert Heathcote's Amato and Colonel Peel's Ion. Although well placed at Tattenham Corner, he faded in the straight. He then won the Ascot Gold Cup carrying the infinitesimal weight of 6 stone 10 pounds, two races at Goodwood and the Grand Duke Michael Stakes at Newmarket. These victories seemed to give Lord George 'folie de grandeur' and he continued writing to all and sundry telling them how they should conduct their racing affairs. An inveterate letter writer he was too blind to realize that to gentle, kindly men such as the Duke of Richmond, who detested letter writing almost as much as he loathed interfering in the affairs of others, the flood of correspondence received from Bentinck was anathema. Typical of the deluge sent by Lord George in dictatorial vein was:

'House of Commons
Aug. 14. 1838.

My dear Richmond,

Write forthwith to Weatherby in your capacity of Steward of Brighton Races authorizing him to hold back the Brighton stake until the objection taken to Louthenbourg's pedigree and identity at Goodwood is decided.'

Louthenbourg had won the 1838 Goodwood Stakes and Lord Suffield, who owned the runner up, objected to Louthenbourg on the grounds that his breeding was misrepresented. The misrepresentation concerned the fact that in 1834 an Epsom trainer had entered a colt to race at Epsom in 1836 as 'colt by Camel out of Fancy by Phantom' whereas the colt in reality was 'colt Louthenbourg, by Mameluke, dam by Smolensko out of Miss Chance'. The Marquess of Exeter, as Steward of the Goodwood meeting, asked Lord Jersey and Lord Wharncliffe to undertake an inquiry.

Mr. Theobald, owner of Louthenbourg, refused to allow his stud books, containing entries concerning mares owned by Mr. Holbrook who bred Louthenbourg, to be examined. The outcome of the case was discussed at a meeting of the Jockey Club in October. Members were asked to decide on a question of Racing Law:

'Mr. Theobald's horse Louthenbourg having won the Goodwood Stakes this year, and the pedigree under which that horse started in 1837 having been ascertained to be a false pedigree by an investigation which has taken place since the race, is Louthenbourg thereby disqualified and the second horse St. Luke entitled to the stake?'

It was agreed that those members of the Jockey Club who were not interested in the race, under the chairmanship of the Duke of Portland, should consider this point. Of the 13 members 8 voted that Louthenbourg should not be disqualified, and thus the stake was paid to Mr. Theobald.

This decision did not, however, stop Lord George from writing to the Duke of Richmond an involved and detailed letter proposing that the unfortunate Duke ought to attempt to gain redress for losing a race to the sire of Louthenbourg eight years previously!

In addition to the problems caused by Louthenbourg at the 1838 Goodwood meeting, spectators saw for the first time in England the great Irish horse Harkaway and his owner Thomas Ferguson. Little could any of the onlookers have guessed that within six years Ferguson would be an important figure in one

47

of the greatest scandals the Turf has ever known—a scandal dominated by Lord George Bentinck.

Ferguson was born in Ulster, and began by working in a linen factory. He was brusque and self-opinionated, but a fine horseman. He soon tired of the dreary life of a factory and after moving to Rossmore Lodge, on The Curragh, became one of the most famous steeplechase riders, trainers and breeders of the era. Harkaway's grand-dam, Miss Tooley, had been bred by Lord Derby at Knowsley in 1808 and shipped to Ireland by a Co. Fermanagh cattle dealer who, having sold a cargo of bullocks in Liverpool, went to Knowsley and spent the total proceeds of the sale on buying Miss Tooley.

In Ireland Miss Tooley won several races before being bought by Lord Cremorne. Sent to stud she bred six foals, one of whom, named Fanny Dawson (also the name of one of Lord Cremorne's daughters!), became the dam of Harkaway and was given by Lord Cremorne to Thomas Ferguson as a present. Sent to Economist in 1834 she dropped Harkaway, who spent his early days on a Westmeath farm roaming amongst the cattle being fattened for the Liverpool market. Although described as a chesnut, Harkaway was really a pale yellow sorrel, with a white blaze on his face, and his near fore foot white to the fetlock. When he matured he was a magnificent looking thoroughbred, deep and powerful in his shoulders, and a great weight carrier. Like so many exceptional horses he was beaten first time out, but between September 1836 and June 1838 he ran 23 times at The Curragh and won 18 of his races. His first venture in England was in the Tradesman's Cup at Liverpool on Wednesday 18th July 1838. He had only just arrived after a bad crossing of the Irish Sea and lost by half a length to Lord Eglington's St. Bennet, to whom he was giving a stone and who had shown he was a top-class handicapper by winning the Northumberland Plate the previous month. Harkaway pulled up lame, but Ferguson insisted on running him again the next day when, once more, he was second.

He was then put into one of the new-fangled horse caravans and taken to Goodwood where he won the Gold Cup, starting at the short price of 5–4 against. Before the race some paddock critics described him as 'a clumsy overgrown brute' and after

8. 5th Duke of
Richmond

9. 5th Duchess
of Richmond

11. Charles Greville, cousin of Lord George Bentinck

10. Colonel Peel

his victory as 'an animal of wonderful power'. Later in the afternoon Ferguson asked if he might present the Gold Cup to the Duchess of Richmond, but the offer was declined on the grounds that it might set a precedent. Ferguson took Harkaway to Wolverhampton where he won the Cleveland Plate, followed by another success at the Doncaster St. Leger meeting. At Wolverhampton on the eve of the race so many gathered around to see 'the great chesnut' that Ferguson charged them sixpence each to see his horse!

Misguidedly, Ferguson now decided to run Harkaway at Lord Wilton's Heaton Park meeting, with the inevitable result, he got beaten, and beaten decisively, for although the record books state that he fell, the general impression was that he was knocked over. His final engagement of the season was at Chesterfield when he walked over.

Ferguson, who suffered from gout, could at times be the victim of violent outbursts of temper, and loathed being crossed. He made no secret of the fact that he was not prepared to let Harkaway win unless he was able to get his money on at a reasonable price, and there can be no doubt that on occasions Harkaway's jockey was instructed to lose. Ferguson and Lord George Bentinck took an immediate dislike to each other, and towards the end of the year, when the Irishman thought that Bentinck had stolen the market in backing Harkaway, he announced angrily 'by God, the public must understand that Harkaway is my hope to win money for me, and not for any damned fellow, either a lord or a thief by the curse of God!'

In 1839 Harkaway was sent to Goodwood where he won the Cup for the second year in succession. Second in the race was a three year old named Hyllus, who ran in the name of Mr. Lichtwald, who every year bought horses from Tattersalls and had them shipped to Germany. Harkaway was now the one horse that everybody, including Lord George Bentinck, wished to buy; Mr. Tattersall even having a commission to purchase him for shipment to America. Ferguson adamantly refused to sell him, and when pressed to name a price stated 'the price of Harkaway is 6,000 guineas, and I hunt him twice a week'. After Harkaway's Goodwood victory the followers of racing were shocked to learn of the dissention of the interested parties with regard to bets made on the race. According to a John Somers, Ferguson had not a single bet on Harkaway when he arrived on the course the day before the race, except for a modest £29 to £4 that Harkaway would win both the Cheltenham and Goodwood Cups. When it was pointed out to Harkaway's owner that there were others who had already backed his horse heavily, he told Somers that unless he was given the odds of 3–1 to £500 he would promptly scratch Harkaway. This news was given in the Swan Hotel in Chichester during the evening and a Mr. Wakefield consequently agreed to allow Somers on Ferguson's behalf £600–£200 Harkaway. Ferguson's reputation was well known and the thought that Harkaway might be scratched without any compunction was substantiated by the fact that a few weeks earlier, Ferguson had ridden the hot favourite at an Irish race meeting, laid heavily against his chances and then ridden the colt straight into the sea!

The next day, at the races, Wakefield spoke to the Stewards and repudiated the bet on the grounds that Ferguson had not given Somers authority to act on his behalf. A month later at the Doncaster St. Leger meeting two of the Jockey Club Stewards, Col. George Anson and the Hon. H. Rous, intended to hear the evidence, but as Somers' witness, although present at the meeting, did not attend, the case was postponed until the Newmarket meeting.

Further confusion was caused at Doncaster by the Clerk of the Course receiving a letter nominating Harkaway to run for both the Queen's Guineas and the Cup—but the letter was not from Ferguson who, when he discovered the attempted fraud, categorically stated that Harkaway would not run. Harkaway was eventually sent to stud where his claim to fame rests on his son King Tom, whose daughter St. Angela became the dam of St. Simon, owned by the 6th Duke of Portland.

6

Throughout the summer of 1839 Lord George was busily engaged in attempting to get Bloomsbury, the winner of the Derby, disqualified on the grounds that he was not the horse he was purported to be. The Derby was run in appalling conditions with snow showers, heavy overnight frost and a cold east wind turning the May day into an afternoon of winter's devilment. To everyone's surprise an unconsidered outsider, Bloomsbury, in the name and colours of Mr. W. Ridsdale, won by two lengths from Mr. Fulwar Craven's filly Deception who two days later won The Oaks. Bloomsbury's dam, Arcot Lass, was also the dam of St. Giles who had won the 1832 Derby for William Ridsdale's brother Robert, who for many years had been racing partner of John Gully, and of Scroggins, second to Elis in the 1836 St. Leger. There was some doubt as to the interest that Lord Chesterfield had in Bloomsbury, for on the bankruptcy of Robert Ridsdale Arcot Lass was bought by him. Two days after the Derby Craven objected to Bloomsbury, giving as his reason the fact that his pedigree was incorrectly stated, and that Tramp and not Mulatto was his sire. The confusion was caused owing to the chaotic inaccuracy of the Stud Book, and Weatherbys casual reliance upon records sent to them by breeders from all over the country. The Epsom Stewards, Sir Gilbert Heathcote and Baron de Tessier allowed the objection to be raised, but the following week sent their decision to Weatherbys stating that in their opinion Bloomsbury was qualified to start for the Derby and that his owner was entitled to the stakes.

This decision infuriated Bentinck, who had persuaded Craven

to go a step further and serve a legal notice on Weatherbys not to hand over the stake money, amounting to a little over £4,000. At Ascot Bloomsbury won two races, the Ascot Derby and a Sweep-stake, but Lord Lichfield, aided and abetted by Lord George objected and requested that the matter was investigated by the Stewards of Ascot Races. A subtle point now arose, for several of those who were to have been called as witnesses refused to appear. The Stewards could not enforce them to do so, and consequently Lord Lichfield decided to abandon any thought of gaining a ruling from those in authority in the racing world and resort to a civil action.

The case was heard before Mr. Baron Maule and a special jury in Liverpool. Baron Maule had a great sense of humour and understanding, and in one trial showed sympathy to a man accused of murdering his wife, after he had calculated that the prisoner who had lived in a small village, had listened to 156 sermons a year from the same preacher for 34 years. The Judge's comments on this fact enabled the accused man's counsel to put in a plea of 'insanity'.

After one of Lord Chesterfield's stud grooms had given evidence, followed by Mr. Cattle, the original owner of the mare Arcot Lass, the Duke of Richmond who had made the long journey from Goodwood, and Mr. Batson were called to prove the Rules of the Jockey Club. Whilst addressing the jury, Ridsdale's counsel was constantly interrupted by his adversary, counsel for Lord Lichfield. Standing this barracking no longer, he said 'I shall not allow myself to be interrupted again by my learned friend without complaining to the Bench. He has frequently, in the course of this inquiry, interposed in a very irregular manner, but I can understand what he wants. He sees he is riding the losing horse, and that I am looking like a winner, and he hopes that by calling me, he will make me look back, and perhaps my nag will go on the wrong side of the post.'

When Baron Maule summed up he began by stating that the Rules of the Jockey Club required that where a mare was covered by more than one horse, the fact should be described in the entry for a race of the particular horse of which she was the dam. The question was not whether Arcot Lass had been covered by

Mulatto, but whether or not she had also been covered by Tramp. If she had been covered by Tramp then the Jockey Club rules had not been adhered to, and Bloomsbury must be disqualified.

In less than an hour the jury found for Ridsdale, and Bloomsbury remained the winner of the Derby and the two Ascot races.

The late summer and autumn of 1839 saw the beginning of Lord George's greatest triumphs on the Turf as an owner. He now possessed a prodigious number of horses in training, as well as mares and stallions including Bay Middleton. One of his objects in entering all his yearlings for countless races, even though the amount he paid in forfeits was colossal, was to bamboozle his fellow owners and bookmakers as to which were his best and which were his worst. He was undoubtedly considered by those who wished to flaunt the authority of the Jockey Club as their strongest opponent, and if in his opinion they attempted to defraud, he did not hesitate to try to defeat them. He despised any form of failure, and after Lord Chesterfield's horse Don John had won the 1838 St. Leger virtually unbacked he remarked 'If I had such a horse as Don John I would not have left the last card seller in Doncaster with a rag to his back'.

Within a year he possessed one of the greatest fillies known in Turf history, but ironically she was so outstanding that, as a betting proposition, she did not avail her owner to any great extent, except when she won The Oaks. Lord George Bentinck had attended the Tattersalls' sale of the virtually bankrupt Lord Chesterfield's bloodstock in 1837 and bought the twenty-year-old mare Octaviana and her filly foal by Priam. The filly was Crucifix, who left the Day family gasping by the brilliance of her trial gallops at Danebury. They realized that they had a world-beater in their hands and that their problem was to keep her ability a stable secret. However the news leaked out and so great was her reputation that many shrewd judges had backed her to win the July Stakes at Newmarket, which was her debut, several days before the race. This did not please Lord George, who ordered John Day to contact the trainers of the other runners and offer to scratch Crucifix if they would guarantee her owner half the prize-money. His object in doing this was to defeat those whom he considered had stolen his market and also to keep Crucifix for another engagement two days later. At the last moment it was decided to run Crucifix who won hard held by two lengths, and thus incurred a nine pound penalty for the Chesterfield Stakes.

There was a false start to the Chesterfield Stakes and most of the runners, including Crucifix, ran the length of the course, with Lord George's filly finishing second to Lord Albermarle's Iris, before they were recalled. When the race was re-run Crucifix won impressively. She then raced at Goodwood, winning the Lavant Stakes and the Molecomb Stakes. Rested until the autumn, she won five races at Newmarket, the Hopeful Stakes, a walk-over for a 100 sovereign sweepstake, and a fortnight later the Clearwell Stakes and the Prendergast Stakes, before dead-heating with General Yates' colt Gibralter for the Criterion Stakes. In all these races she started odds-on, and on each occasion Lord George doubled her up to win her race and the next year's Oaks.

She began her three-year-old career by winning both the 2,000 Guineas and the 1,000 Guineas. The hard ground in the early summer jarred her legs, and it became certain that The Oaks would be her final race. This news was kept secret by Bentinck, not only before the race, but also after it, so that he could take advantage of the fact that she was favourite for the St. Leger and highly unlikely even to go to the post. The Oaks was an extra-ordinary race, for there were sixteen false starts which caused a delay of more than an hour. Crucifix was badly away on the ultimate occasion, and had the hardest race of her career before winning by half a length. One of the best racing fillies of the century, she was not attractive to look at, and one contemporary described her 'standing nearly sixteen hands high, she had a neck long and light. Her shoulders were thin, her chest very narrow indeed and her legs small. She was flat sided, with short back ribs and drooping quarters. She is said to have been a shambling mover with a tendency to cross her legs, but she was as active as a cat, and had the faculty of reaching her top speed in a few strides.' Another contemporary describing her owner at this time wrote 'Lord George Bentinck is a lion of the Turf and a very dangerous customer. He is a profound calculator: an excellent judge of a horse—spares no expense in training, running and in keeping up his stud from the best blood, and will some fine morning give the Ring such a shaking as will make it tremble or fly in pieces. He goes for the great coups and has never been known to suffer any familiarity at the hands of any of the low squad.' Surprisingly he seems to have taken very little note of the 1840 Derby winner Little Wonder, sent down from Berwick-on-Tweed to win at 50–1, even though there seems justification to believe that Little Wonder was a four year old, masquerading as a three year old.

Before the end of the year Captain Rous had been appointed by the Duke of Bedford to take over the management of his horses at Newmarket, and to be responsible for the engaging and matching of the Duke's horses. Rous, who had been elected a Steward of the Jockey Club in 1838, found this new task completely to his satisfaction—especially as he was to stand in for one quarter of the stakes every time a match was made. Two things were less to his liking: the high-handed manner in which Lord George Bentinck behaved in regard to his relationship with others on the Turf, and his own election to Parliament in 1841. For the next five years he was member of Parliament for Westminster, but the atmosphere of the House of Commons was not suited to his temperament, particularly as he cut a poor figure as a public speaker.

Lord George Bentinck did not have a runner in the 1841 Derby, won by the favourite Coronation. Belgrade, the first horse that Levi Goodman had run in the Epsom Classic, was well backed but finished in the ruck. In the paddock before the race Lord George paid scant attention to either horse or owner—but within three years the name of Goodman was to merit far greater consideration from him. At the Liverpool Summer meeting, Lord George, who for some years had insisted that the starts of races were appalling, and the starters biased and inefficient, and had recommended and instituted improvements, was criticized for allowing his own horse Misdeal to start 50 yards in front of every other horse. Misdeal had won the race easily, but the incident was made ugly by the fact that the starter had been Lord George who was also one of the Stewards of the Meeting. The result of the race was allowed to stand after evidence had been heard by the other Stewards. In order to vindicate the ability of Misdeal, Lord George ordered him to be started in the final race of the meeting, and beforehand told all and sundry, including the bookmakers, that his instructions to his jockey were that he should start at least two lengths behind every other competitor. These instructions were obeyed, and Misdeal proved her owner's point by romping home lengths ahead of his rivals. Misdeal was ridden by Howlett, the Day's apprentice. Lord George had the first retainer on him and John Day, who paid Howlett's father £80 a year, took all the apprentice's earnings. A contemporary wrote: 'At the great race-meetings Lord George Bentinck invariably occupied a private lodging, and might have been seen, when the Ring was broken up, lounging on the course, or about his paddocks, accompanied by his trainer, but seldom or ever in Society. Familiars he had none, and though completely free from hauteur of bearing, and accessible to all in the way of business, no man knew better than he how to preserve dignity with urbanity, or to parry an attempted liberty by a look. His usual dress at these meetings were buckskin breeches made from the hides of his own stags, top-boots, a buff waistcoat and a reddish brown double breasted coat ornamented with the Jockey Club buttons, and a beaver hat from under which his auburn hair protruded.'

In August Lord George went to Ireland, ostensibly to visit Ferguson at Rossmore Lodge. There was a possibility that Ferguson would sell him a horse called Tearaway, but the deal did not materialize. Whilst at Ferguson's stables Lord George was impressed by two young horses, Fireaway, half brother to Tearaway, and Goneaway, whom he thought both bigger and more backward than Fireaway. Lord George never trusted Ferguson, who openly admitted his dislike for the Duke of Portland's son. Nevertheless the two men had at least one interest in common—their determination to keep the best of the odds about their fancied horses for themselves.

At Doncaster in the autumn Bentinck was responsible for the settling of a dispute between the Corporation of Doncaster and some of the aristocrats who patronized the St. Leger meeting. The Town Clerk had rejected a proposal that there should be four instead of five days racing, and another suggestion that during race-week it would be more profitable to stage one Ball instead of two. He added that the Corporation were prepared to increase their grant from £400 to £500. Bentinck, with his love for statistics and comparisons, pointed out that the revenue derived from the racecourse by the Corporation was greater than that derived by any other Corporation in the kingdom, whilst their contribution to the race-fund was less than any other. For the years 1820–40 Doncaster Corporation had received an average of £2,000 annually, and subscribed a mere £400 a year to the race-fund. At Liverpool, where Mr. Lynn had spent more than £20,000 on his grandstand, £1,600 a year was subscribed to the race-committee. At Chester, with 5 days racing, £940 was contributed, whilst at Ascot £950 was the sum involved, with a bonus of the proceeds of admission to the grandstand being added to the race-fund. In comparison to these financial arrangements, the sum offered by the Doncaster Corporation was parsimonious. Bentinck's diatribe resulted in the Corporation offering a further 200 guineas to the race-fund—an offer scornfully dismissed with the threat that unless they could do better the gentlemen who patronized the meeting would go elsewhere for their sport. In the light of this threat, a meeting of the Town Council was held in the evening, and a subscription of £1,000 a year to the race-fund was agreed upon.

Towards the end of the year Lord George took his horses away from Danebury and sent them to John Kent at Goodwood. The news of his intention was given to Kent at the Newmarket Houghton meeting, and if it caused the Goodwood trainer, renowned for his loyalty and integrity, no surprise, it clearly involved him in an immense amount of extra work. The rift between Lord George and the Days at Danebury had been growing wider for some time, largely due to the suspicions in Bentinck's mind that his horses were being trained by the Days for their financial advantage and not his. In his opinion this was unforgivable and outweighed his love for Danebury as a training centre. For some years he had thought nothing of posting from London to Andover, resting for a few hours, and then riding on to the gallops at dawn to see his horses at exercise. After a day of discussion about the horses he would return to London and go immediately to the House of Commons, frequently without bothering to change his clothes.

The racing stables of the Day family, sheltered amidst beech trees at the foot of Danebury Ring, were situated four miles north-west of Stockbridge. Although the Downs were bleak and windswept, it was an ideal area for the training of horses for the white chalk soil retained enough moisture in summer to keep the turf soft and springy, whilst in winter the ground never became waterlogged. Consequently the gallops offered almost perfect going at all times of the year. Stockbridge racecourse adjoined the Danebury stables and the Day's horses used the race track for much of their fast work. Over 100 people were employed in the care of the horses and the maintenance of the gallops under the watchful eyes of the Day family. Sam Day and his brother John had learnt the art of jockeyship at Newmarket, Sam spending six years with Cooper who trained for the Duke of York, and John being apprenticed to Smallman, the Prince Regent's trainer, at an annual wage of ten pounds and two suits of livery. Sam Day rode three Derby winners, in 1821 on Gustavus, 1830 on Priam and 1846 on Pyrrhus the First, but his brother, although successful five times in The Oaks, never rode one. For many years John Day both rode and trained at Danebury, ruling the stable with a strictness which compelled obedience and secrecy. Every Sunday the stable lads were made to go to church twice, and then listen to bible lessons in the dining-room. Anyone not paying attention felt the lash of John Day's whip across his shoulders. In 1834 Pussy was sent out from Danebury to win The Oaks and was the first of the many Classic winners trained by the Days. Lord George Bentinck loved the peace of the Hampshire countryside, but he also loved the isolation of the Danebury stables which were virtually inaccessible for touts. Crucifix, Grey Momus and Chapeau d'Espagne were trained at Danebury and Lord George also sent his stallion Bay Middleton to stand there after he bought him from Lord Jersey. When Lord George took his horses away from Danebury, a confederacy was formed by the Days, John Gully, who lived at Bishop Waltham near Winchester, his son-in-law Pedley, Joshua Arnold a bookmaker, a London bill discounter named Turner and Harry Hill, Bentinck's erstwhile commission agent.

Obviously the move of all the Bentinck horses from Danebury to Goodwood caused a great deal of ill-feeling, and as the last horse left Danebury the stable lads jeeringly shouted out that the entire collection of horses were not worth the cost of the move. Their insults were proved wrong, for amongst Lord George's horses taken by Kent to Goodwood were his Liverpool winner Misdeal, who in 1842 won the St. James's Palace Stakes at Royal Ascot, as well as races at Goodwood and Newmarket, Firebrand, who won the 1,000 Guineas, and Gaper, an unbroken yearling of whom Lord George had the highest opinion and hopes.

During the winter of 1841-2 Lord George devoted his energy and initiative to turning the Goodwood stables into the best in the kingdom. The Duke of Richmond was fired by Lord George's enthusiasm, and willingly gave permission for him to carry out his every wish and whim. Kent at times did not know whether he was on his head or his feet as an endless stream of commands, requests and instructions on stable ventilation, feeding, drinking and training innovations poured forth in endless profusion from Bentinck's pen. Trees were cut down, banks levelled and new gallops made, upon which tons of mould and tan carted from Chichester were laid. Describing Bentinck at this time Kent wrote 'He was invariably dressed in a long frock coat, a black or very dark blue double-breasted velvet waist-coat and dark trousers, having in the fashion of the day, straps attached, which he passed under his boots. Over his waist-coat he wore a fine long gold chain, which went around his neck, and was clasped together on his breast by a gold loop, in which was set a large and very conspicuous turquoise, which I always regarded as symbolizing his sky-blue racing jacket. Round his neck he wore a costly cream-coloured scarf of great length, knotted under his chin, with a gold pin stuck in it. This gold pin contained either a big ruby or a pearl. In this costume Lord George was always dressed when he went round the stables at Goodwood.'

During the first three months of 1842 Lord George and his father were involved in a case which threatened the authority of the Jockey Club. The matter had started some six months earlier when a bookmaker named Gurney had been unable to settle his commitments over the favourite's victory in the 1841 Derby, until he received money from his debtors. It was proposed by his creditors, and agreed to by the Jockey Club, that Gurney's affairs should be placed in the hands of 'three persons of high respectability' who would settle Gurney's debts out of monies which they would attempt to collect from those who owed money to him. A fortnight after the Derby, certain members of the Jockey Club, including Rous, Peel, Anson and Greville, met at Weatherbys and agreed that 'Messrs Portman, Beales and Clarke, being authorized by Mr. Gurney to settle his Epsom account, and having undertaken to do so on the payment of the sums due to Mr. Gurney, all persons indebted to Mr. Gurney are bound to pay the amount of their debt to these gentlemen.'

A copy of this decision was sent to Tattersalls, and Portman, Beale and Clarke attempted to collect money from Gurney's debtors.

Amongst those who owed Gurney money was Lord George Bentinck, who refused to have anything to do with such a compromise—much to the consternation of his fellow members of the Jockey Club. Bentinck took the view that he could not recognize the doctrine that money owed to Gurney should be paid to a third party with no guarantee that the winners would receive the amount of their claims. He also considered that the decision had not been taken at a formally convened meeting of the Jockey Club, and that some of those who had signed the declaration were 'interested parties', which made it invalid. Therefore, he was not prepared to settle the amount of his loss unless the assignees guaranteed that the creditors be paid in full at some definite period. When the assignees gave their undertaking that the account of Mr. Gurney would be paid in full by the end of the Houghton Meeting, Bentinck settled his losses and expressed his hope that other debtors would follow his example. The Houghton Meeting passed without full settlement being made, and Bentinck wrote to the Stewards of the Jockey Club bitterly reproaching them for their attitude to the affair.

One of those who refused to settle his debt to Gurney was a

Mr. Thornton, who was sued by Gurney in the Court of Exchequer. The Judge, Lord Abinger, deliberately explained to the jury that they were concerned solely with a legal dispute and they were not concerned with any Jockey Club ruling. They found in favour of Thornton. The Jockey Club decided that as Thornton refused to pay his debts he should be warned off Newmarket Heath and consequently informed their tenant, the Duke of Portland, that it was his duty to serve the requisite notice on Thornton. It is highly likely that if he had not been influenced by Lord George the Duke would have done this without more ado, particularly as after the Jockey Club had warned a man named Hawkins off Newmarket Heath in 1827 the Duke had successfully brought an action for trespassing against him.

However, Lord George felt that here was an opportunity to flaunt the Jockey Club, many of whose members he considered to be incompetent, and in consequence the affair became one of acute embarrassment to all concerned—except for Lord George himself who revelled in the fact that his father refused to comply with the Jockey Club's demands. In February 1842 he wrote to the Duke of Richmond from his father's London home:

'Harcourt House
Feb. 3. 1842
Thursday night

My dear Richmond,

I propose calling upon you tomorrow morning at ten o'clock if that will suit you for the purpose of considering the course to be taken at the meeting of the Jockey Club on Saturday. It is very important that anything we do should be previously well considered, for I understand that never was half the Whip made for any Government or Opposition that has been made on this occasion by the Stewards—& I hear on all sides & have heard for some days past from people unconnected with racing that there would be far more excitement about the meeting of the Jockey Club than about the meeting of Parliament so we must mind what we are about—I believe the Publick out of doors is with me, the members of the Jockey Club against me.

Very sincerely yours
G. Bentinck'

This was followed up by a further frenzied letter ten days later, less than 24 hours after he had misguidedly sent a letter to the *Morning Post* criticizing the Jockey Club.

'Harcourt House.
Feb. 13, 1842

My dear Richmond,

The thing is done, I sent my protest to the Morning Post last night & I have no doubt it is in type by this time.—Whatever I might have been disposed to do under other circumstances the blackguard conduct of Charles Greville & the unhandsome conduct of Rous & George Anson in making the comments that they did upon Thornton & all those who appealed to Courts of Law (which they well knew applied equally to if not meant for me) after the conciliatory tone I had taken towards them would utterly prevent my sparing them & those who asked with them in any way.

In regard to the Jockey Club if it proceeds in the course in which it has of late been proceeding, the sooner for the sake of the Turf it is abolished the better. There is no good in such an assembly, in fact it is an absolute nuisance.

This is the third time that Rous by deciding matters in his own favour in which he had a pecuniary claim has raised a general War amongst the members of the Jockey Club—viz—the Louthenburg case—and the Bloomsbury case—his vicious example instead of being avoided has been imitated—where then do you gather your hope that by submitting to these proceedings of the Jockey Club you will obtain any reform in their general conduct.

Yours ever most sincerely
G. Bentinck'

Lord George's long protest sent to the *Morning Post* and published in full, contained twelve points. The letter concluded 'Lastly, a defaulter of notorious wealth wanting only honesty & principle to pay his debts of honour, is the last species of defaulter around whom the Jockey Club ought to throw the shield of its partial & paternal protection.'

Two months later the Stewards of the Jockey Club held a meeting especially to discuss Lord George Bentinck's letter to the *Morning Post*. It was one of the most heavily attended meetings that there had been in the history of the Club, with 33 members present. Colonel Anson began by stating that it was the opinion of the Stewards that Lord George's letter assailed the Jockey Club in very strong and offensive language. He concluded by requesting permission to leave the Chair as the conduct of the Stewards was in question, and moved that the Duke of Beaufort should deputize. Lord George then spoke to his fellow members and stated that he was anxious to conciliate the goodwill of the Club, and whilst adhering to all the principles and maxims of the Turf Law laid down in his protest letter, he was desirous to express his regret for the language in which the letter had been couched if it had given offence to the feelings of the Club. This apology was considered acceptable by the members of the Jockey Club, and the matter ended.

There followed six weeks of correspondence between the Stewards of the Jockey Club and the Duke of Portland on the subject of warning Thornton off Newmarket Heath and the Duke's responsibilities as the tenant of the Jockey Club. It was clearly the intention of the Jockey Club to assert their authority, and equally clearly the intention of the Duke, influenced by Lord George, to oppose them.

Even after a considerable number of letters had been written by the Duke of Bedford and Colonel Anson to the Duke of Portland, behind the scenes Lord George Bentinck was still determined to stir up trouble, particularly with regard to the part that Colonel Anson had played concerning Gurney and Thornton. He had persuaded his father that Anson had acted wrongly over the debts of Gurney, and although Anson persistently explained that he had held a guarantee from Lord George Bentinck in a private capacity, the Duke of Portland was persuaded that Anson had accepted a guarantee in his capacity as a Steward of the Jockey Club. Much to the Duke's consternation and that of the Jockey Club the affair became common knowledge in the London clubs, largely due to Lord George's garrulity. The Jockey Club were thoroughly disgruntled by Lord George's behaviour and the Duke of Bedford wrote to the Duke of Portland explaining that '. . . nobody expects him to humble himself, or to retract his opinions, or to do anything derogatory to his character, but he is expected to withdraw the harsh words . . .' The next day Bedford wrote again proposing that Lord George should compose a letter withdrawing his protest. This would enable the Stewards to announce that the matter had been satisfactorily settled. It seemed the most sensible solution, and Lord George duly sent off his 'humble pie' letter. The Stewards, however, did not consider that the letter constituted adequate regret and Bentinck wrote to the Duke of Richmond '. . . all negotiations with the Stewards are off . . . the Duke of Bedford's colleagues declined to ratify the treaty and this put an end to all amicable arrangements.' It did not, however, end all amicable arrangements between the Duke of Portland and the Jockey Club, for at the end of July Charles Weatherby received a letter from the Duke suggesting that he would be willing to sell them his estate in the parish of Burwell for £10,000. If this proposal did not prove acceptable for the reason that the Jockey Club could not raise the ten thousand pounds, the Duke was willing to lease the estate for a period of thirty one years for £2,000 and a rent of £250 per annum provided the rent was paid to anybody in London that he might name.

Colonel Anson, who had taken so much trouble to mollify the Duke of Portland in this matter, was rewarded by seeing his colt Attila win the Derby. Nevertheless the 1842 Derby was not without incident for the *Sunday Times* published two articles attacking Colonel Peel and Charles Greville for scratching their horse Canadian at the last moment. The implication was that the owners gained substantially from betting transactions by withdrawing Canadian. In August a libel action was heard before Lord Abinger at Croydon with Mr. Thesinger appearing for Colonel Peel and Mr. Greville, and the Solicitor General for the *Sunday Times*. Lord George Bentinck as well as the Dukes of Portland and Richmond were subpoenaed by the defendants, but were not called to give evidence. Damages of £250 were awarded against the *Sunday Times* and probably appeased Greville, who shortly after the Derby had written:

'The racing and racehorses and all things appertaining thereto, the betting, buying, selling, the quarrels and squabbles, the personal differences and estrangements, the excitement and agitation produced by these things, have had the effect on my mind of

64

13. Admiral Rous and George Payne

12. Sir Frederick Thesiger

14 and 15. Goodwood House and (*below*) the library

withdrawing my attention from public affairs from literature, from society, from all that is worth attending to, and caring for, from everything that is a legitimate object of interest, and wasting my thoughts, faculties and feelings on all that is most vile, most worthless and most morally and mentally injurious.'

Also on Greville's mind was the happy news that his niece, Frances Harriet, was to marry the Earl of March, son of the Duke of Richmond. Less happy were his continual disagreements with Lord George which were causing their mutual friends much embarrassment. The antagonism of the cousins which had started years previously over trivialities such as each giving conflicting instructions to their jockeys and the winning of Preserve at Goodwood, had festered during Crucifix's two-year-old career, and had eventually grown into undisguised enmity.

Although Grey Momus had failed Lord George in 1838, in the winter of 1842–3 he began, once again, to wonder whether it might not be his turn to stand beside the victorious colt in the winners enclosure after the Derby, for in Gaper he owned a horse who had shown immense promise as a two year old. Sired by his own stallion Bay Middleton, Gaper had won the important Criterion Stakes at Newmarket in the autumn of 1842. Notwithstanding this victory, Lord George did not consider it morally wrong to announce that Gaper was a doubtful starter for the following year's Derby in the hope that such an announcement would lengthen the odds. Kent, the trainer of Gaper, was convinced that he was a top-class colt, but was pessimistic of his soundness for, almost without exception, horses sired by Bay Middleton broke down in training, and to make matters worse, Gaper seemed to pull up lame after every strong gallop. At what stage in the winter months Lord George began backing his colt is uncertain, and it is doubtful if his commissioners were able to get more than a modest amount on, for at the end of March Gaper was quoted at 50–1 and a month later at 100–1 at Tattersalls. More significant was the steady backing of Levi Goodman's colt Maccabeaus who for some time was second favourite for the Derby.

Gaper's first race of the 1843 season was a match, which he won, at the Newmarket Craven meeting. Two days later he won another sweepstake, but it was an unimpressive victory and disappointed Lord George. The bookmakers also thought less of Gaper's Derby chance and he drifted further out in the betting. Kent, however, remained hopeful although, like others who had been at Newmarket, he had a high regard for Cotherstone who had won the 2,000 Guineas. Cotherstone, owned by John Bowes, whose Mündig had won the 1835 Derby, had been defeated by Gaper at Newmarket as a two year old, but during the winter had improved tremendously, and at Malton, where he was trained by John Scott, he was considered a champion. Yet the nearer that Derby Day loomed, the more confident did Lord George become that Gaper would win.

His commission agent, Harry Hill, backed Gaper so heavily that on Derby Day his price had shortened to 5–1 and Lord George, who stood to win more than £100,000, is reputed to have exclaimed: 'I'd feed Gaper on gold if that would ensure his victory'.

Bentinck's attention to the Derby was diverted momentarily by a request from John Gully who was frantically trying to learn news of his son whom rumour suggested had been murdered in the Far East, after a shipwreck. Gully thought that Bentinck could use his influence at the Foreign Office to discover if the rumours were true.

A few days before the Derby an attempt was made to 'nobble' Cotherstone, but to no avail, and the culprit was caught in the stables with a bottle containing vinegar in his pocket. Cotherstone's claim to favouritism was obvious, and even Queen Victoria and Prince Albert went to Mickleham to see him have one of his pre-Derby gallops. Much as Lord George fancied Gaper's chance he backed the favourite to save his stake on Gaper and show a profit. In the Derby, although Gaper made much of the running and was shouted as the likely winner once the straight was reached, he faded inside the last two furlongs and finished fourth to Cotherstone. Sam Rogers, Gaper's jockey, was criticized for making so much use of him in the early stages of the race, and a despondent Lord George wrote to Kent a week after the race, not only complaining that he would lose £1,600 by bad debts, but also wondering if Gaper would have run better if the Derby had been a fortnight later.

There can be little doubt that Gaper was not a sound horse, and the Duke of Richmond jokingly suggested that if Gaper's portrait was ever painted, the artist should have him standing in straw to conceal his legs. Nevertheless Gaper ran 15 times as a three year old and won seven races, which offset to a small extent Bentinck's racing expenditure, for he owned over seventy horses, including foals and yearlings and 28 horses in training who ran in 122 races during the season. His bill for training fees came to over £7,000. After Gaper's final race, Lord George wrote to Kent:

'I was in hopes that Gaper would have retrieved all his lost laurels today, by winning his last and 15th race & thus have given some eclat to Bay Middleton, but the iron hardness of the ground and running a severe race yesterday I suppose has made him sore and he cut a sorry figure today—'

At the July Goodwood meeting Colonel Anson tried to end the feud between Bentinck and Charles Greville who hoped for a reconciliation with his cousin. Anson arranged for the two men to meet, but at the last moment Bentinck changed his mind and walked away, refusing even to shake hands.

7

The entire question of the legality of betting, and the authority of the Jockey Club to enforce its rules outside a Court of Law was rapidly coming to boiling point. Its prolonged altercation with the Duke of Portland had eventually resulted in a strengthening of its power, but only at Newmarket.

As a member of the Jockey Club Lord George Bentinck was determined to prevent defaulters from escaping their financial obligations, but his efforts were not always successful, and judgement was given against him in the case he brought against an owner named Connop, who had entered three horses for the 1842 Duke Michael Stakes at Newmarket. The conditions of the race were such that it cost 50 sovereigns to enter—and Connop refused to subscribe the 150 sovereigns he owed to Lord George, whose horse had won the race. His refusal was based on an obscure statute of King Charles II which enacted that no action in horse racing could be maintained to recover a stake in excess of £100. It infuriated Lord George that men such as Connop should be able to avoid settling their debts by hiding behind these statutes, and he considered it outrageous that they were supported by the law in their efforts to avoid their liabilities. The case was not heard until the end of 1843, and Lord George commented on it in a letter to Michael Benson, who had requested permission of Bentinck to dedicate his annual calendar to him. In granting permission, he suggested that Benson included the Connop judgement in his Racing Calendar for he believed that the judgement would expound the whole law on the subject of how stakes ought to be drawn up to be recoverable from dishonest parties.

He added that he thought that all Stewards of Races, and pro-prietors of Race Stands should include 'Swindlers and Cheaters', as well as defaulters amongst those prohibited from entering stands and racecourses, and in particular notices to this effect should be printed on each ticket of admission, as was done at Liverpool and Goodwood.

The end of 1843 found Bentinck more involved both politi-cally and on the Turf than at any time in his life. He was now 41 years of age, unmarried, in good health, and obsessed with his crusade to rid the Turf of the villains and blackguards who attempted, by fraud and deceit, to make racing a mockery in the eyes of honest men. England as a nation seemed tired of gambling and debauchery, and with the coronation of the young Queen and the birth of her son Albert Edward in November 1841, a new era dawned. The solid prosperity and strict morality of the middle classes seemed to ring the death knell to the decadence heralded some 50 years previously by the advent of the Prince Regent and his circle of admirers.

Although Lord George Bentinck clamoured against the skull-duggery which existed and flourished on the Turf, largely due to inefficiency and incompetence, he was not averse to stooping low in his own efforts to score financially at the expense of others. If he thought there was a horse at Goodwood sufficiently well handicapped to merit a large bet, especially at long odds, he would go to extremes to cloak his activities. The secrecy with which Red Deer was prepared for the Chester Cup of 1844 was a typical example. As a two year old, the Duke of Richmond's Red Deer had run so badly at the Goodwood meeting that he was offered for sale to his jockey Sam Rogers, who refused to buy a horse he thought useless. In the autumn Red Deer, ridden by Kitchener, who only weighed 3 stone 4 lbs, began to improve and in trial gallops defeated some of the Goodwood two year olds who had won races. In all home gallops he consistently beat another of the Duke's horses, Pastoral, who showed his ability by winning at Newmarket. After the race Pastoral was claimed, and Kent had some difficulty in buying him back. Returned to Goodwood Pastoral was tried once more against Red Deer who won more easily than ever. It seemed as though Red Deer must land a betting coup the following year, and Bentinck wrote to Kent in elated mood outlining his plans for betting on the Chester Cup. As a subterfuge he proposed entering five of his horses for the Cup in addition to Red Deer, so that the bookmakers would not know which was the stable's intended runner. He would then back 'Kent's lot' to win £5,000 and hoped that 'by betting against each of the others as they come up, to make the stable stand to win on Red Deer to the losing of nothing, but to affect this object not a guinea must be laid on Red Deer singly. I think that if Lord March keeps his own counsel and does not let others into the stable secret. . . .'

The same evening Lord George wrote again to Kent in a furious temper:

'There is a conspiracy going on to get Kitchener away from me, composed of Mr. Drinkald, General Wyndham's friend and neighbour, John Day and Mr. Wreford, and they are prepared to give the boy's father £100 a year for the use of the boy and his earnings . . . No time must be lost in getting the boy's father to Goodwood and arrange the terms of the contract by which I must agree to give the boy so much a year for three or five years in consideration of which he must be bound to ride 1st for me, 2nd for the Duke, 3rd for Lord March. . . .'

Kent was hardly allowed a moment's peace and in January 1844 received a note from Lord George in very unusual vein:

'I have got a line that Mr. Harris of the Royal Hotel, Chichester, is to be sold up on Monday next, and if I do not look very sharp all my goods & chattels now left there will be sold with the rest for the benefit of his creditors. My goods are:—

a large bath tub painted green outside and white inside
2 large wash handbasins, & jugs
a large bed mattress
a pair of fine linen bed sheets.'

Poor Kent was expected to collect these items. Bentinck also complained to Kent about Lord March:

'Of course I shall take no notice of what you tell me of Lord March being dissatisfied with the manner in which I have put him on when the horses in the stable have been backed—I could however tell a very different tale which my books would show.

I very much doubt if any other instance can be found of so much favour being shown as has on every occasion been shown to the Duke & Lord March to my own prejudice in allotting the odds when the horses in the stable had been backed.'

By the time the Chester Cup took place in the early summer of 1844, Red Deer was a heavily backed favourite—and won like a handicap certainty. Immediately after the race homing pigeons were despatched from the race course to Goodwood giving the news of Red Deer's victory and when Red Deer's horse-box arrived from Chichester the stable lads unharnessed the post horses and jubilantly drew the van containing Red Deer up to Goodwood House.

Inevitably Lord George found enemies amongst those whose nefarious racecourse activities he tried to ruin. Not all the gamblers, the cheats and the defaulters, although afraid of his autocratic power, were prepared to be broken without a struggle. They imagined that they would be given support, indirectly, by William Crockford who was better informed than any other man in England concerning the frauds and swindles which made certain horses 'dead meat'. The defaulters had another notable ally in the law—for no matter what action the Jockey Club took, the Courts would not recognize gambling transactions or enforce their settlement. However in 1843 a small-time crook by the name of Russell, aided and abetted by others more influential and more reluctant to enter the limelight, served writs on certain members of the Jockey Club including Lord George Bentinck, Charles Greville and Colonel Peel, under an obscure statute of Queen Anne which commenced with the words 'Qui Tam'. The statute provided that any amount in excess of £10 which was won or lost by betting could be sued for and recovered, together with treble the amount so won or lost, at the suit of a common informer. It was in consequence of this statute being invoked that the Duke of Richmond was hurried into introducing his 'Manly Sports Bill' into the House of Lords, by which the obsolete statute was repealed and its penalties abolished. The Bill was not introduced until February 1844, and for a time during the winter it seemed to Lord George Bentinck that there was a grave danger of Russell succeeding in his action and he viewed the affair with alarm. He did all in his power to make the others who had been issued with writs realize the dangers of the situation. One of them was John Bowes, who, although the son of Lord Strathmore, never succeeded to the title as he was born many years before his parents married. He was an immensely rich man, by nature shy and retiring, and seldom went to race-meetings, but he bet heavily on his own horses in races such as the Derby, and won over £20,000 in wagers as a result of Cotherstone's Epsom victory. He was perturbed by the writ served on him by Russell and wrote to Bentinck asking for his advice. Lord George replied from Harcourt House on November 8th 1843:

'. . . It is quite true that I am in the same predicament with yourself in regard to having been served with notices of action for penalties to the amount in my case of £62,500 incurred under the 9th of Queen Anne for excessive and deceitful gaming by reason of betting on horse-racing.

At first I and my solicitors were alike disposed to hold these threats very cheap and to look upon them as idle attempts to extort money—but I am sorry to say that upon examining the matter more closely they have entirely changed their note and think it a very serious matter.

There is doubt the vagabonds have the law on their side and our only chance of defeating them is by their failing in their proofs or by our throwing them over on some technicality. At the same time there is no doubt they will find it no easy matter to get all the proofs necessary to a conviction before we must fain hope an unwilling Jury. In the meanwhile I have put the matter in the hands of my regular solicitors . . . . . . and with Follett to ride the horse prepared by them, the Devil himself must preside in person over the proceedings of his satellittes if you do not succeed in defeating their unholy gang of Hellkeepers who are the fellows really moving in this matter acting as I am told under the guidance of Jos. Anderson and some add Jim Weatherby.

Russell the informer, I believe keeps a Hell called "The Strangers" and is himself a Turf Defaulter having cut a run at Wolverhampton—Peel, Charles Greville and Eglington have all got notices similar to yours and mine.

Our first endeavour must be to procrastinate as much as

possible in the hope of getting the trials postponed beyond the meeting of Parliament, when we must see if we cannot get an Act passed at once staying proceedings and permanently altering the Law . . . .'

Bentinck was worried that the Russells—referred to by him as the 'Infernal Alliance'—had managed to retain the Solicitor General whose power he considered to be almost omnipotent. He attempted to wrest him from them but failed to do so, and for a time was greatly perturbed that his opponents should have such an eminent legal figure on their side. He had been served with six writs, but was convinced that before any case could be heard the law would be altered. He also admitted to John Bowes that 'I have registered a vow in heaven to take signal vengeance upon these scoundrels and please God to favour my pursuits of these said devils half of them shall be exterminated by the time . . .
. . . I hear that the two Russells—the Informer and the Uncle Attorney were prowling last Thursday night for upwards of an hour and a half in front of Crockfords and at last had the audacity to walk absolutely into the vestibule evidently looking out for some person whom they wanted to serve a writ—it is clear therefore though they may with a view to putting us off our guard give out amongst their pals that they do not mean to proceed that in fact they do intend to go on with the actions. . . .'

In his next letter, dated December 11th, Bentinck wrote:
'Judgement has not been given either in my case or Greville's, and this being the last day of the Court sitting Judgement cannot now be given at earliest before the 11th of January so we shall have no new light thrown on the subject by the Judges. I am sorry to say, however, that the more I look into the case and the more I study the innumerable trials which have taken place on the subject of bets & stakes the more satisfied I am that we have no safety but in an Act of Parliament—and therefore no time must be lost in agitating both sides of the House to procure the passing of a new Law on the subject. There seems more reason than before to believe that Jim Weatherby has something to do in the matter. . . .'

Three days later, Bentinck sent further information to Bowes who was in Paris. '. . . a distringas has been granted to force you to

73

make an appearance upon the writs already served . . . there is no use now in your playing hide and seek any longer—therefore I think you would do more good if you were to come over to England and agitate for a repeal of the law. I am sorry to say I hear that Lord Palmerston expressed a doubt whether Parliament could be induced to pass such a law . . .' In another letter written on the last day of the year Bentinck stated '. . . it is certain they (the Infernal Alliance) will have all the information young Weatherby can give them (this I learned from the reporter of the Sunday Times who called upon me yesterday and informed me that in October Jim Weatherby himself told him he would be revenged upon *me* in particular for the part I had taken in excluding defaulters) and they will have all the information Whitfield can give them which Hill doubted until last Friday upon happening to go late at night into Evan's in Convent Garden who should he find there but Whitfield and Russell the Informer sitting 'tête à tête' together smoking cigars over their brandy & water! This makes it clear that whatever Whitfield's evidence will avail we shall all be in great jeopardy, but beyond this at present I have not ascertained that any spirit of treachery prevails in the Ring.

With respect to getting a bill things do not look so pleasant at present. Nothing is settled and upon my going to Sir James Graham on Saturday last my interview was far from satisfactory—he said in the first place it was a very delicate matter for the Government to touch—that anything like protection to betting on Horse-racing would be quite sure to rouse up indignation and opposition of all the Saints in both Houses of Parliament and especially of the Bishops in the Lords: that before he could even meddle with the matter a formal representation must be made to him either by the Jockey Club or from a large body of the great supporters of the Turf of both parties (i.e. Whigs & Tories) praying for the interference of the Goverment to stay proceedings and to alter the law; this done he will bring the matter under the consideration of the Government and take the opinion of the Cabinet upon it. In the mean time, strange to say he stated that if we were to come now to the Government, the Government would answer "What proof have you that the Law is against you. The Act has been in force these 130 years and no 'qui tam' action

has ever been enforced under it for betting on horse-racing . . ."
Follett gave it as his opinion if he could have the opportunity of
trying the first case *for the Defendants* that he should succeed in
defeating the actions—but so far from speaking with any confidence on recommending us to stand the brunt of any action he
strongly urged us by all means "to be up and doing" without
loss of time to get a bill passed before any verdict was obtained
which in his opinion would greatly increase instead of facilitating
the passing of any remedial act.

Sir James Graham, on the contrary, treated the matter just the
other way and began by saying "till some action was decided against
us there could be no just ground for any interference by Parliament"
and upon my saying that interference after Eglington had been
successfully sued for £68,000, you for £30,000, and me (through
Hill) for £12,000 would be locking the stable door after the steed
was stolen, he at last consented to say that then we must get the
current opinion of all the leading men at the bar including the
Attorney General and the Solicitor General, and if they gave a
concurrent opinion as to the bearing of these Statutes on Horseracing and that having fortified ourselves with such opinions and
got also a formal Memorial drawn up and signed by the principal
Members of the Turf praying for the Government's interference,
he would then lay the matter before Sir Robert Peel.

The difficulty of all this proceeding lies in the scattered state
of the Members of the Turf and in the great difficulty in calling
together any meeting at this time of year; and also without such
a meeting and some agreement growing out of it to make common cause in regard to expense how is so serious a matter to be
satisfactorily arranged? Probably 150 guineas would be required to get the legal opinions referred to—these Conferences
of great Lawyers are fearfully expensive; at present, I am the
only member of the Turf moving in the matter and I quite tremble
at the thought of my solicitor's bill as far as it even now has gone—
but certainly I cannot, neither do I think, that you, Eglington &
I together ought to bear all the expense of proceedings taken and
adopted for the general safety of the sporting community. At the
same time I do well know the selfishness of mankind and above
all of that portion of it which constitutes the Jockey Club that

I am quite sure that unless some previous arrangement is made they as a body will leave the whole business and expense upon those who fight the battle. . . .'

The Earl of Eglington, to whom Lord George referred, was a fine athlete and was renowned not only as a gentleman rider and crack shot, but also for his prowess at billiards, racquets and curling. He also showed an interest in the new-fangled game called golf, admired by those who lived at St. Andrews. He had inherited his title on the death of his grandfather in 1819, and although he did not fritter away his fortune at Crockford's he was content to gamble heavily on his own horses if he thought they had an outstanding chance. When his filly Blue Bonnet won the 1842 St. Leger he collected over £30,000 from the bookmakers, and it was as a result of some of these bets that he was issued with writs in the 'Qui Tam' actions. The Earl drank nothing but champagne throughout meals, and on one occasion in the Jockey Club Rooms at Newmarket he announced that he could drink more champagne at a sitting than any other man alive. It was a rash pronouncement which led to a match for £25 a side against Sir David Baird, brother-in-law of Colonel Peel; the conditions of the match being that as soon as one man had drunk a bottle, his rival should finish his and two more bottles be produced and drunk—this procedure to continue until one of the drinkers admitted defeat. To his surprise and consternation Eglington was beaten and whilst the next morning he was seen in Newmarket High Street beating his head and crying out for a chemist, Sir David Baird played three games of billiards with Squire Osbaldeston before going to bed and was seen on the Heath watching the horses exercising a few hours later.

Bentinck sent a final letter to Bowes on January 10th 1844:

'Our Bill and Memorial and Historical Precis of the Laws which affect betting on sporting matters are all prepared now. . . . Our bill simply repeals the obnoxious clauses in the Acts of the 16th Charles II, 14th Anne, and 18th George II and nothing being said about staying proceedings or costs all actions though even a verdict of a Jury were obtained will fall to the ground upon our bill being passed unless the penalties have been actually levied— and of course if the "Infernals" were to be such fools as to go on with their actions after they saw the Bill successfully progressing through Parliament all we should have to do would be virtually to have judgement arrested by going into the form of a nominal appeal to the House of Lords—You have done wisely in taking care that Lord Brougham should be told that the Duke of Richmond has already got charge of the Bill—for it seems by universal consent of all the world that the Duke of Richmond is the fittest and the most influential man to bring it forward. . . .'

The Memorial mentioned by Bentinck was commented upon in an article in *The Times* on January 30th 1844:

'The Statutes against Horseracing. A copy of a memorial, intended to be presented to Parliament immediately upon its meeting, for the repeal of the statutes against horseracing, has lately been handed about in sporting circles. Numerous "qui tam" actions have been commenced by a certain clique for the recovery of penalities to an enormous amount from persons of the highest distinction, as well as others who have been for years unsuspiciously betting on horseracing, coursing, etc., and who, it would seem, under the statute of Anne and Charles, are liable to be sued for amounts involving ruinous consequences. The memorial sets out first the advantages derived from horseracing in the maintenance and improvement of the breed of horses, for which this country has so long been celebrated, and the serious and rapid deterioration which would be the consequence of any discouragement of the sport. There is then a statement of the number of racehorses kept in this country, the amount of plates run for, and the taxes paid to the Government upon racehorses. It then states, that although gaming has been at all times discouraged and punished as regards card playing and such-like gambling, yet that horseracing ought never to be allowed to come under the definition of gaming, for the bets are chiefly made for the purpose of repaying the owners of horses the extensive outlay that has been made. The memorialists say that the suppression of betting can never be properly effected, and that legislative enactment is the only means by which just and equitable stakes can be upheld and fraudulent and deceitful practices prevented.'

When the Duke of Richmond moved the second reading of the Manly Sports Bill in the House of Lords, the Bishop of London stated that whatever advantages might result from the promotion of manly sports and pastimes, if they were to be purchased at the expense of facilitating betting by the removal of legal restraints he would feel bound to oppose the Bill. In answering the Bishop, the Duke pointed out that his object was to destroy fraudulent betting, and added that although he himself never bet, he believed that unless the existing system of betting was checked, the Turf would soon be deserted. He continued that as the law stood, no one could play a game of cricket where the loser paid the expenses without rendering himself liable to a 'Qui Tam' action. He added that it was his hope that land near large towns be put aside for manly pastimes and amusements—for it was better that they should go there than to the beer shops where they became sullen and discontented. Lord Brougham, Lord Campbell and Lord Denman also gave their views concerning the Bill. Lord Denman, who had given judgement against Bentinck in 1842 proposed that a Select Committee be set up to consider the whole future of the Gaming Laws. In replying to Lord Campbell, who had suggested that all bets should be considered debts of honour, the Duke explained that the difficulty was to decide how to treat those fellows of no character who repudiated their debts of honour. He continued that if one of their Lordships bet that he would go to Palace Yard and meet twenty lawyers in their wigs in the course of an hour, this bet could be recovered, but a bet on a racehorse was not recoverable unless the racehorse ran for nothing.

When the Bill was discussed again on Monday February 8th the Duke of Richmond was absent, and Lord Brougham pointed out that in his opinion the 'Qui Tam' actions had been brought by certain parties out of spite because they had been excluded from associating with the respectable gentlemen who had formed themselves into clubs where arrangements were made for carrying on horseracing. Only the Bishop of Exeter spoke in disagreement to the views expressed by Lord Brougham, before the Bill was read a second time.

The passing of the Manly Sports Bill and the setting up of the Select Committee virtually defeated the infamous Russell. Nevertheless one case—against Lord George Bentinck—was

heard at Guildford Assizes on August 8th 1844 before Mr. Baron
Parke and a jury. As soon as the case started the Judge demanded
of Russell's counsel—Mr. Platt—as to why the case was being
brought when the recent Act of Parliament had 'stayed all proceedings in all actions which may have been begun at the period
of its passing'. Mr. Peacock, counsel for Lord George Bentinck,
rose to his feet and dramatically announced that the defendant
was most anxious for the case to be tried, and added that when
Lord George Bentinck had voted in favour of the Act, his vote
had been objected to, and he had decided not to avail himself of
the Statute in the approaching trial. There was further opening
drama when a Mr. Bovill rose to explain that he had been briefed
to appear on behalf of some of the witnesses subpoenaed for the
plaintiff, and pleaded that his Lordship had not the power to
try the case. The unfortunate Mr. Bovill was given short shift
by the Judge who explained that it was impossible for the Court
to hear any arguments on behalf of witnesses. The crux of the
case was the question of bets made by Lord George Bentinck
and also bets made by John Day over Gaper in the 1843 Derby.
Day who had seen Gaper as a yearling at Danebury was convinced that he would not win the Derby and laid £20,000 to
£250 in the course of the Spring. On the morning of the Derby
Gaper's price had so shortened that Day lost his nerve and asked
Harry Hill, Lord George Bentinck's commission agent, if he
could 'hedge' his bet. This was done—to the extent of £20,000–
£3,000 so that from Day's viewpoint if Gaper won the Derby
he would be quits, and if he lost, then he would be £2,750 out of
pocket.

When John Day was called as a witness, Mr. Bovill jumped to
his feet and told the Judge that in his opinion Mr. Day should
decline to be sworn—giving as his reason that anything he might
say would almost certainly jeopardize any action taken at a later
date about bets he had made. A bewildered Day was then told by
the Judge 'You are not bound to answer any questions which will
render you liable to any penalty. . . . You must allow me to exercise my judgement as to which questions you should answer. . . .
Where you lost a bet you must answer, where you won a bet is a
different thing . . .' For the next half hour confusion reigned as

John Day vacillated, forgot, became absent-minded and ultimately admitted that it would have been far easier to remember with whom he had made wagers if he had his betting book with him. Unfortunately he had lost it. The next witness was Harry Hill, who by sheer coincidence had also lost his betting book which made it difficult for him to state categorically the details of his 1843 Derby transactions. The celebrated John Gully was then cross-examined and lent weight to the defendant's case by stating that the bets he had made with John Day, Hill and Lord George Bentinck were all separate and had no bearing on each other. In his summing up the Judge explained to the jury that their decision rested upon whether or not they thought that John Gully had acted as Day's agent. If they thought this, then they must find for the plaintiff, Russell. If they thought that Gully's bets were on his own account they must give their verdict in favour of the defendant. When their verdict in favour of Lord George Bentinck was announced there was 'a slight demonstration of approbation which was instantly suppressed'.

16. Lord George Bentinck's Grey Momus, winner of the 1838 Two Thousand Guineas

17. Bay Middleton, the 1836 Two Thousand Guineas and Derby winner, bought by Lord George Bentinck from Lord Jersey

18. Colonel Peel's Orlando, awarded 1844 Derby on the disqualification of Running Rein

19. Lord George Bentinck's Crucifix, winner of the 1840 One Thousand Guineas and Oaks

8

The frauds perpetrated in the 1844 Derby were the culmination of
the crimes, substitutions, deceptions and swindles which had
beset racing England since the end of the Napoleonic wars. They
originated four years earlier at Malton, the most famous racing
and hunting centre in the north of England. For generations
training grooms had galloped their masters' horses on Langton
Wolds. A Malton-trained horse won the 1780 St. Leger, and two
years later Imperatrix owned by a Prebendary of York Minster,
and also trained at Malton, repeated the triumph when he won the
final Classic to the delight of all Yorkshire. The greatest era in
Malton's history came with the advent of the Scotts who in 1825
bought Whitewall, a training establishment with boxes for about
25 horses. Soon there were more than 100 racehorses trained
there, out of the total of 1,200 trained throughout the land.
Between 1827 and 1863 John Scott, the most skilful trainer in
England, sent out the winner of six Derbies, sixteen St. Legers,
nine Oaks, six 2,000 Guineas and four 1,000 Guineas. His owners
included Lord Chesterfield, Colonel Anson, Mr. John Bowes and
Lord Stanley. He and his brother William, who rode four Derby
winners, three Oaks winners and nine St. Leger winners, were so
celebrated that Whitewall was described as 'The mecca of the Turf'.

Yorkshire revered the Scotts although the brothers were not
Yorkshire bred. Their father had lived at Chippenham, a small
village near Newmarket, where he had trained horses for Sir
John Lade, friend of the Prince Regent, and it was not until they
were young men that the Scotts came to Yorkshire. Their hospitality was on a lavish scale and European Princes, members of

the Jockey Club, and a certain Baron Alderson, a renowned High Court Judge, would visit Whitewall to see the great trainer, to watch the gallops on the Langton Wold, and in the evening to reminisce about past victories over gargantuan meals and decanters of port. In later life John Scott used to say 'I would rather be hanged on Langton Wold than feasted at Newmarket'. Yet, although the Scotts of Whitewall were the most renowned of the Malton trainers and their horses the best, there were plenty of other trainers including Henry Stebbings, who looked after some of Squire Osbaldeston's horses at nearby Ebberston. Stebbings, born in 1817, was a man of violent temper and his views on honesty and integrity far below those held by John Scott. Stebbings had lived at Hambleton near Malton all his life, and had worked with horses ever since he was a boy. Like many others who found it difficult to make both ends meet financially he was willing to act as horse groom, dealer, trainer, agent, tout and informer in order to profit by his knowledge of racehorses.

One of the men who from time to time employed Stebbings was Abraham Levi Goodman, who lived in Foley Place, London. Goodman typified the sharp practising villains of the Turf whom Lord George Bentinck loathed. Plausible and astute, he kept horses entirely for financial gain, and would go to any lengths to bring off a betting coup. His mind concentrated on devising fraudulent schemes, and he spent time and money in acquiring racing information from men such as Stebbings.

In September 1841 Goodman bought a yearling at Tattersalls' Doncaster sales. The yearling was 'a bright bay, no white, black legs and good eyes' bred in Yorkshire by Sir Charles Ibbotson, and foaled in April 1840, by Gladiator out of a mare by Capsicum. It was hoped that the foal would prove to be a top-class horse and before Goodman bought him Sir Charles Ibbotson had entered him for the 1843 Derby. His sire Gladiator, who had been second to Bay Middleton in the Derby of 1836, stood at Althorp near Northampton at 20 sovereigns a mare and a guinea the groom. The fee was to be paid before the mares were taken away, and it was stated that any mares not removed by August 1st would be sold by public auction to defray expenses. Sir Charles Ibbotson was the most honourable of men, and little dreamed of the

82

nefarious plans that Levi Goodman had for his yearling. After Goodman acquired the Gladiator yearling he was turned out on George Worley's farm near Northampton for the winter. It was intended, originally, to call the colt Prizefighter, but as Lord Chesterfield owned a horse of that name, Spartacus was chosen as an alternative, before, ultimately, the name Maccabeus was decided upon. In January 1842 Maccabeus cut and lacerated his leg, and a veterinary surgeon, Mr. Gurling, was called in to examine and treat the injury. The injury was not serious but it was evident that there would be a permanent scar.

At Newmarket in the autumn of 1841, a month after he had bought Maccabeus, Levi Goodman told Henry Stebbings that he was on the look-out for one or two foals, and in consequence Stebbings bought a colt foal by The Saddler out of Mab for 28 sovereigns on his behalf. One peculiarity inherited by the colt from his sire was cracked heels, but this did not deter Stebbings from buying him.

The Saddler was a tough brown horse with the blood of Eclipse, Highflyer and Matchem in his veins, who had started favourite for the 1831 St. Leger after victories at Northallerton and York. Although failing to win the St. Leger he was bought by Squire Osbaldeston and won the Doncaster Gold Cup in a canter before being sent to stud at Ebberston, where he proved comparatively successful as a sire. The colt foal that Stebbings bought, was bred by Doctor Cobb, a Malton surgeon, who in June 1840 decided to send his bay mare Mab to The Saddler, whose stud fee was 10 guineas including a guinea for the groom. Young Thomas Lofthouse took the mare over to Ebberston and saw her covered by The Saddler. Mab dropped her foal the following May. He was a shabby, thin and slight bay colt with four black legs and feet, and a few white hairs on his forehead and, although born rather late, was described as 'a smart little fellow' because of his stout limbs. All summer the foal and his dam were turned out in a paddock at Doctor Cobb's house where they were cared for, not only by Thomas Lofthouse, but also by the seventeen-year-old John Kitchen, a servant of the doctor, who helped in the stables, ran errands and in the summer helped on the farm. In the early spring of 1842 Goodman instructed that the yearling, named Running Rein, was sent by train to London. Stebbings' younger brother James took the colt to the railway station at York and travelled with him on the train to Euston, from whence he was taken to stables close to Langham Place.

In the year 1842 the Langham Place area included the homes of surgeons, physicians, dentists and architects. Sir Gilbert Heathcote, a member of the Jockey Club owned an imposing house in Langham Place, and so too did the Countess of Mansfield and Sir Theodore Brinckman. In adjoining Dorset Square lived two Major Generals and the Portuguese Consul General, but the streets and mews leading off the Square were a rabbit warren of stables and smaller dwellings which were the homes of cabinet makers, upholsterers, plumbers, book-binders, carpenters, bakers, grooms and horse-dealers. Horses were constantly coming and going and little notice was taken of any young racehorses stabled alongside the carriage horses. Levi Goodman's brother-in-law, Mr. Joseph, kept stables in one of the streets off Dorset Square and on Goodman's instructions he sent an employee, Daniel White, to collect Running Rein from Euston station and take him to Chapel Street Mews, also off Dorset Square, where Goodman maintained a stable. Two days later Running Rein was taken to the livery stables of James Pearl in Milton Street also near Langham Place where he was kept for 10 days, before being sent to William Bean at Finchley. Bean had been a horse-dealer for more than 30 years, twice had been made bankrupt and twice insolvent. Whilst at Finchley Running Rein met with a slight accident when he tried to jump the fence between his paddock and the adjoining one. He damaged his near foreleg and the skin was grazed from his knee. Future events were to prove that this injury may not have been an accident at all, but a deliberate attempt to ensure that both Maccabeus and Running Rein had similar scars.

On 24th September 1842 Daniel White was sent down to Finchley once more to collect Running Rein. Bean was rather surprised to get a note from Levi Goodman handed to him by White ordering the removal of the yearling, and even more surprised when White casually said that he was going to the local pub for a drink and that Running Rein could be brought to him there. Some ten minutes later the horse was produced and taken by White back to Levi Goodman's stables in Foley Place and later in the afternoon, to the livery stables of John Haines, who was a friend of James Pearl, and kept the Portman Arms in Milton Street. The transferring of Running Rein from one stable to another was part of Goodman's deliberate intention to confuse anyone who attempted to trace his movements. At the same time as Running Rein's arrival at Haines' mews stables from Finchley, Goodman arranged that Maccabeus should also be sent to Haines. The journey took three days, with stops for the night at Woburn and St. Albans.

Two days later, on Goodman's orders, Running Rein and Maccabeus and another colt were taken to William Smith, an Epsom trainer. In October 1842 the three horses were broken by George Hitchcock, a man of great experience who, at a later date, admitted that although he had been told that all three horses were yearlings, he thought that one of them could have been a year older. He was reluctant to mention this to Smith for, on a previous occasion when he had suggested that a horse sent to him was a year older than was claimed, Smith had lost his temper and horsewhipped him.

It is impossible to determine when Levi Goodman first decided to switch horses in order to perpetrate the fraud of attempting to win the Derby with a four year old, but it is almost certain that it was before his colts went to be trained at Epsom in the autumn of 1842.

If the fraud was successful the fortune to be won was so great that a certain amount of risk was worth while. The ability of a good four year old in the summer months was such that, at level weights over 1½ miles, he was virtually certain to defeat three year olds—the only horses eligible to run in the Derby. The problem of the fraud was how to substitute a four year old for a three year old, without causing suspicion. There were so many people involved in the care of a horse from its birth onwards that to produce an unraced four year old to compete in the Derby was exceedingly unwise.

Another difficulty was that the winning prize-money of about £5,000 was infinitely less than the amount to be won from successful ante-post bets made at Tattersalls throughout the months preceding the race, on a fancied and proven Derby candidate. If substantial sums of money were wagered on an unraced and unknown horse, questions would inevitably be asked, which might lead to undesirable investigations. Details such as the breeding and name under which the horse was entered also had to be considered, particularly as entries for the Derby closed two years in advance. Goodman, with both guile and a comprehensive understanding of racing, came to the conclusion that his best chance of success would come from not only confusing the issue by a trail of false clues involving more than one horse, but also by producing his potential Derby winner in two-year-old races, when in fact he was a three year old. The crux of this scheme was that if the horse seen in the Epsom paddock on Derby Day was recognized as the same horse as had been seen and accepted racing as a two year old the previous season, there was less likelihood of an inquiry into the identity of the horse. Goodman relied upon the incompetence of racing authority who could be hoodwinked without difficulty, and also on his own ingenuity.

Goodman had made up his mind that Maccabeus should impersonate Running Rein in two-year-old races at the end of the 1843 season and also in the 1844 Derby, but that did not solve the problem of what to do in the meantime. If Maccabeus, liberally entered in races for three year olds throughout the 1843 season, did not put in an appearance, questions might be asked as to what had happened to the horse. Equally if he ran in the spring as Maccabeus and in the autumn impersonating the two-year-old Running Rein, even more difficult questions might be asked by knowledgeable race-goers who thought that they recognized the horse. Goodman decided, therefore, on a daring addition to his plans. He would buy another horse to impersonate Maccabeus! If the scheme succeeded, it would be masterly, for the racing world including Bentinck, Gully, Crockford, and those who wagered at Tattersalls would be lulled into false security. Goodman, described by one contemporary as 'the wily Jew with several ugly blots and not a few mysteries to account for' contacted Harkaway's owner, Thomas Ferguson, whom he had met at

Goodwood in July 1842. The Irishman agreed to lease him a colt named Goneaway for 12 months for the sum of £500 (in fact Ferguson received £400 and an IOU for the balance), each of them to take half any winning stakes. Goneaway arrived in Liverpool in January 1843 and was immediately sent to Haines' stables in Langham Place, where both Maccabeus and Running Rein had been housed four months previously.

Goodman left Maccabeus and Running Rein with Smith at Epsom until February 1843 when he peremptorily ordered their removal to his own secluded paddocks at Sutton. Here they were joined by Goneaway, who was prepared by Goodman's trainer, William Sadler, for a race at the Epsom Spring Meeting, a sweepstake of 5 sovereigns each, with 50 sovereigns added by Sir Gilbert Heathcote. Levi Goodman nominated Maccabeus as his entry for the race but it was Goneaway who impersonated Maccabeus and was beaten into second place at the astonishing price of 7-4 on in a field of 13! One cannot help wondering to what extent the secret had leaked out. Goodman had cut Goneaway's tail and procured a dye from a London chemist with which he had painted a white pastern to make Goneaway and Maccabeus look even more similar, but the starting price was so ridiculously short that the possibility that the bookmakers knew of the substitution is not unjustified.

During the summer months it was given out that Maccabeus was dead. No horse ran again during the year in his name, but it has been suggested that Goodman intended to run Goneaway as Maccabeus in the 1843 Derby, for which he was at one time during the spring second favourite. Unfortunately Ferguson arrived unexpectedly in England and Goodman realized that if he saw Goneaway at Epsom the substitution would be disclosed—consequently the horse disappeared. It is almost certain that Ferguson took Goneaway back to Ireland. What happened to him after that is pure conjecture. What is not conjecture is that Levi Goodman was fined in June for non-attendance on a Criminal Court jury; he had gone to Ascot races!

Goodman now owned two unraced horses, both of whom had the similarity of a scar on their knee and both of almost similar appearance—the difference being that the Gladiator colt

Maccabeus was a three year old, and Running Rein a year younger. Nothing more was heard of the two horses, who were kept with other of Goodman's horses at Sutton, until the autumn when on Monday October 9th Maccabeus, masquerading as Running Rein, made his debut at Newmarket in a £50 Sweepstake. There were 12 runners and Running Rein, who started favourite at 3–1, won comfortably by 3 lengths, a result which would not have caused a surprise to those who knew that a three year old was defeating two year olds. The next afternoon in the Clearwell Stakes, Running Rein ran again, and finished third to Colonel Peel's filly Zenobia.

Meanwhile Lord George Bentinck had persuaded the Duke of Rutland, whose filly had finished second in the Clearwell stakes, to lodge an objection with the Stewards of the meeting on the grounds that the winner was a three year old. All summer Lord George had been suspicious that Goodman was trying to switch a horse, and having seen Running Rein at Newmarket he was convinced that his opinion was correct, for the horse not only looked far too big and muscled up for a two year old, but won too impressively. If the Stewards had decided to hold their investigation immediately the objection was lodged, Goodman might have been caught out. However they agreed to hold the inquiry on the Tuesday of the Houghton meeting—exactly a fortnight later. This delay gave Goodman the opportunity he was seeking, and proved fatal from Lord George's point-of-view. During the fortnight he sent an agent to Malton to make inquiries from Doctor Cobb and others who knew the history of the colt by The Saddler, and also arranged for Kitchen, the lad who had seen the colt by The Saddler out of Mab born at Malton to be brought to Newmarket. Lord George was out when Kitchen arrived but his valet looked after him and gave him bread and cheese for his supper. The following morning, Lord Stradbroke, Charles Greville, Thornhill, Goodman, Bentinck, Kitchen and a veterinary surgeon named Bateston inspected Running Rein in his box, after which Kitchen was taken to the Jockey Club Rooms and interrogated. He had little hesitation in pronouncing that the horse he had just been shown was the horse he knew as Running Rein and had seen at Malton two summers previously. In the circumstances the Stewards announced that the objection was over-ruled, and that the stakes should be paid to Mr. Goodman. As an afterthought, to safeguard themselves, the Stewards added that they did not think Running Rein should ever run again at Newmarket. Bentinck was indignant and was still convinced of Goodman's villainy. In retrospect it is not difficult to imagine how the fraud was perpetrated. Goodman was sufficiently cunning to realize that Bentinck had guessed what was happening, even if he could not prove it. He also knew sufficient about the Stewards of the Jockey Club to gamble that if an objection was lodged, there would be a time lag before the inquiry was heard. This gave him ample opportunity to substitute the two-year-old Running Rein for the three-year-old Maccabeus, who had raced and won at the Second October meeting. The horse Kitchen saw with Lord Stradbroke really was the two year old—but he was not the same horse who had raced a fortnight earlier, for during the fortnight Goodman had surrepticiously brought the genuine Running Rein from Sutton to Newmarket. Surprisingly the veterinary surgeon was not ordered to inspect the horse's teeth, a sure sign of age, but even if he had done so it would not have availed Bentinck, for the inspection would have supported Goodman's contention that the horse was only a two year old.

Goodman's plan had been successful so far. Maccabeus was accepted as Running Rein, and the only problem was to wager as much money as possible upon the outcome of the 1844 Derby. At Christmas John Day's The Ugly Buck and Crockford's Ratan, were joint favourites at 7–1, but Goodman had taken all the available 33–1 offered about Running Rein, whose price had shortened to 20–1. He was far less interested in the honour and glory of leading in a Derby winner than in landing a huge gamble, and as part of his subterfuge decided to sell Running Rein. He sent one of the two horses back to Smith at Epsom in November 1843 and then pretended that he could not settle an outstanding debt of £200, which he owed him for training fees. As Goodman anticipated Smith suggested that Running Rein be sold in settlement—to an honourable and respected Epsom corn merchant Mr. Wood, who supplied Smith's stable and was Smith's landlord. Goodman had made certain that he also was in debt to Mr. Wood, whom he knew to be guileless, and whom he relied on Smith proposing as Running Rein's new owner. The deal was satisfactorily completed with Mr. Wood liquidating the debt and also paying Goodman £200. All parties were satisfied, and looked forward expectantly to winning the Derby.

It seems reasonable to suppose that the horse who arrived at Smith's stables before the end of 1843 was the two-year-old Running Rein, for Lord George was still on the war-path and was capable of descending unannounced on the stable with an expert vetinerary surgeon and demanding to be shown the horse in so dictatorial a manner as would brook no refusal. To substantiate this theory is the fact that in February 1844, when the hullabaloo of the Newmarket Steward's inquiry had died down, Goodman suddenly insisted that the horse at Smith's was sent over to his gallops at Sutton for a trial. One must assume that, whatever happened prior to this trial, it was the four-year-old Maccabeus impersonating Running Rein who returned to Smith's stable at Epsom to be prepared for the Derby.

At the end of February the Newmarket touts watched the Classic candidates as they started the arduous and searching gallops which would break down some and turn others into potential champions. Crockford's Ratan, considered the best two year old of 1843 after his victories in the New Stakes at Ascot and the Criterion Stakes at Newmarket, had not grown a great deal during the winter, but was well muscled up and pleased his trainer by the ease with which he won his trial gallops. Cooper, who trained for Colonel Peel and General Yates had all his three year olds forward in condition, but in their gallops Ionian went better than Orlando. Sam Chifney enthused over Thornhill's string of three year olds—especially Apprentice—and the horses under the care of Boyce also looked in good condition. During the winter the Duke of Portland had taken his horses away from his former trainer Prince, and had become a partner of the Duke of Rutland, but neither of them raced on an extensive scale, owning eight horses between them as opposed to Lord George Bentinck's thirty, some of whom had such unusual names as 'Here I go with my eye out' and 'All round my hat'. The principal danger to the Newmarket horses for the Derby came from John Day's The Ugly Buck, who had won his only race as a two year old, the Molecomb Stakes at Goodwood, with considerable ease. The Ugly Buck had wintered well, and the Danebury gallops had not frozen up during the cold spell which had retarded the training programme of other Classic contenders.

At the Newmarket Craven meeting in April Ratan, who impressed the paddock critics, won a sweepstake over the Ditch mile by two lengths. Sam Rogers rode him with great confidence, and after the race it seemed difficult to imagine how he could be defeated in the Derby for he had beaten high-class horses in the manner of a champion. Lord George had believed him to be the best two year old in England ever since Ascot the previous summer and had backed him heavily for the Derby. What made Lord George uneasy was that Ratan was to be ridden at Epsom by Sam Rogers, who had ridden Gaper for him. After Gaper had finished fourth to Cotherstone in the 1843 Derby, Bentinck had scourged Rogers for incompetent riding, and the blaspheming Rogers had sworn vengeance.

On the first evening of the Craven meeting the betting fraternity went to the newly constructed Rooms which had been built for the comfort of those not eligible for the Jockey Club Rooms. The principal saloon of the 'betting house' was 53 feet in length and 18 feet wide, with Racing Calendars, newspapers and magazines in profusion for the members who used it. The next day Colonel Peel's Orlando won the Riddlesworth, but was not considered to have enhanced his Derby prospects by this victory, although the manner in which he defeated the Duke of Portland's Beiram filly in a match two days later made some spectators wonder how good he might be. Half an hour later Orlando walked over for a sweepstake of 200 sovereigns, for which there had been six subscribers. The bookmakers were still content to make Ratan and The Ugly Buck joint favourites for the Derby, although Orlando had a few supporters. For the most part Running Rein was unquoted and unnoticed, much to Levi Goodman's relief.

The Newmarket Spring meeting a fortnight later opened in glorious weather, with the sun so hot that it seemed like midsummer. The Danebury Classic hope, The Ugly Buck, looked agnificent as he was paraded before the race for the 2,000 Guineas, and started odds on favourite to beat his six rivals. Running Rein had been entered, but did not run, because Goodman had no intention of allowing suspicious race-goers to see him before the Derby. Thornhill's colt Elemi was second favourite, but there was little or no money either for Lord Bentinck's The Devil to Pay, or for Doctor Phillimore, owned by Mr. Maugham, a friend of Goodman. Immediately the race started Sam Rogers drove The Devil to Pay into the lead and set a fast gallop with the intention of trying to run The Ugly Buck off his feet. At the Bushes The Ugly Buck challenged Lord George's colt, with the remainder trailing in the rear. For a few strides the two leaders raced neck and neck until ten yards from the post The Ugly Buck forced his head in front. No one could have been more pleased than Lord George at the result, for he knew that The Devil to Pay was not a top-class horse, and the fact that The Ugly Buck had only just beaten him made Ratan, in his opinion, even more of a certainty for the Derby. Therefore he backed Crockford's horse once again. Later in the afternoon Red Deer, carrying 8 stone 7 pounds, won the Coffee Room Stakes, a wonderful trial for the Chester Cup, in which he was handicapped to carry four and a half stone less. The wagers, already struck, looked gilt-edged. On the evening of the 2,000 Guineas Bentinck wrote to his trainer agreeing to run Croton Oil in the Derby and added:

'Unless there is something wrong—which I very much suspect —with Ratan I expect to see him beat The Ugly Buck very easily for the Derby and to see Orlando second. If Ratan is amiss I expect now to see Orlando—wretch that he is—win the Derby.' Significantly there was no mention of Running Rein. Obviously Bentinck was unhappy about the immense amount of money that he and others had bet upon Ratan and had no illusions about the truth of the remark once made by the bookmaker Jem Bland who, when told by the owner of a heavily backed favourite for an important betting race that his horse was well, replied 'That may be: but I would rather have heard from you that he had broken down, for then I might have profited from it.'

Even after The Ugly Buck's 2,000 Guineas victory, the

Newmarket touts were convinced that Ratan would win the Derby. The three year olds trained by John Scott at Whitewall seemed moderate, and although Sir Gilbert Heathcote's two nominees, Campunero and Akbar, were fancied at Epsom, their form was not outstanding. Sir Gilbert, who lived at The Durdans adjoining the Epsom racecourse, was one of the most popular members of the Jockey Club. At The Durdans he kept a stud of more than 20 brood mares, and two stallions, in addition to maintaining 10 horses in training with Sherwood. As his horses were trained on the Epsom course, it was considered that the horses in his 'crimson, grey cap' had a slight advantage over their rivals when they raced at Epsom due to their familiarity with the track. Sir Gilbert seldom bet, and was reluctant to race his horses further afield than Ascot, Hampton, Egham and Goodwood.

Ratan was favourite at 5–2, The Ugly Buck 9–2, Running Rein 16–1, Orlando 25–1 and Leander 30–1. An unusual price quoted and taken was 1000–500 that Ratan beat The Ugly Buck irrespective of where they finished. There was also a little money for a horse facetiously named Qui Tam.

The Derby was due to be run on Wednesday 22nd May. To Levi Goodman's consternation the previous Saturday a protest against Running Rein signed by Lord George Bentinck, was sent to the Stewards of Epsom Races, and also announced at Tattersalls, where, as usual, in the week preceding the Derby no notice was taken of the Sabbath.

On Sunday afternoon Tattersalls was thronged until nearly 7 o'clock, and on Monday there were so many people anxious to 'hedge' and lay off bets on horses drawn in sweepstakes that it was again evening before the business of the day was concluded. Rumours were spreading regarding the Derby prospect of Running Rein, who became a popular choice even though another protest, signed by Crockford, was lodged objecting to Mr. Wood's horse. At Whites Club the Earl of Glasgow, who had taken a violent antipathy to The Ugly Buck, offered to lay £90,000–£30,000, but there were no takers for so large a wager, although the following morning a fellow member did accept £10,000–£2,000 The Ugly Buck for the St. Leger.

Levi Goodman had hoped that so much attention was being taken of Ratan and The Ugly Buck that his horse might be overlooked in the betting, especially since it had not been seen on a racecourse throughout the spring. There was not the slightest doubt that Bentinck was still smarting under his failure to have Running Rein disqualified at Newmarket in October 1843, and that he would relentlessly pursue his inquiries for two reasons: the first and obvious one was that he wished to rid the Turf of men such as Levi Goodman. The second was that he wished to do everything in his power to ensure Ratan's victory, because of the enormous wagers he stood to win. He knew that if Running Rein was a four year old, then he would surely beat any three year old at level weights. In consequence, as soon as John Bowes and John Scott arrived in London for the Derby meeting Bentinck explained his suspicions about Running Rein and enlisted their support. Bowes was grateful to Lord George for his efforts to defeat the Russells in the 'Qui Tam' actions, and Scott equally disliked any form of dishonesty. Their protest read:

'We, the undersigned owners of horses engaged in and intended to run for the approaching Derby, having strong reason for believing that the horse meant to be started as Mr. Goodman's Running Rein is not the b. colt by The Saddler out of Mab by which pedigree Running Rein is described in his earlier nominations, but some other horse, and one above three years, which has been substituted for the colt by The Saddler, out of Mab, request you as Stewards of the Races to investigate the matter, and to oblige the owner or owners of the horse to prove his identity by evidence, and above all by a proper examination of his mouth by a veterinary surgeon of character and eminence of your selection to satisfy you before he is permitted to start that he is not more than three years old.

And we, the undersigned, hereby engage and undertake to bear you harmless of all expense incurred by any such investigation, and further to indemnify you against the consequences of any action at law which might be brought against you, should you in the discharge of your duty as Stewards think proper to hinder the colt in starting, until you shall have been satisfied that the colt intended to be started as Mr. Goodman's Running Rein is no more than three years old, and the identical animal described in the entry for the Derby. We have the honour to be, gentlemen, your obedient humble servants:—

G. Bentinck
John Bowes
John Scott

To the Stewards of Epsom Races.'

The most significant fact in the protest is that throughout it there is no acknowledgement of Wood's ownership of Running Rein.

One of the Stewards of Epsom Races was Sir Gilbert Heathcote whose London house was in Langham Place. Bentinck thought that he might have heard rumours about the proposed fraud from his servants, who frequented the nearby Portman Arms and had friends amongst those who lived in the mews and stables surrounding Dorset Square. Bentinck quizzed him, but he was unable to confirm any of the rumours. The other Steward was Baron de Tessier who lived at Woodcote Park, Epsom. On more than one occasion the previous year he had seen William Smith's horses at exercise on the Downs, and rumours as to their merits could have reached his ears. The protest instigated by Lord George cannot, therefore, have come as a shock to them, nor can a further protest lodged by Lord Maidstone two days later against Leander, owned by the German brothers Lichtwald, on the grounds that he, too, was a four year old. In 1843 Leander had twice been placed at Goodwood, and had won at Ascot. He, like Running Rein, had been closely guarded during the spring of 1844 and had not been seen in public. To Bentinck's annoyance the Epsom Stewards did very little about the protest, other than to request the owners of Running Rein and Leander to produce certificates showing the breeding of the horses concerned, and to warn them that should either horse win the Derby there might be further investigations and the Stakes withheld. It was a classic example of dilatory expedience, based upon the pious hope that neither would be successful at Epsom and that the affair would therefore, be terminated without further ado. Such reasoning deserved to fail.

On the Monday afternoon before the Derby the annual stall-holders, busily erecting their booths upon the Downs, were shocked by the distribution of a leaflet issued from Scotland Yard: 'All persons playing or betting in any booth or public place, at any table or instrument of gaming, or at any game or pretended game of chance, will be taken into custody by the police and may be committed to the House of Correction, and there kept to hard labour for three months. By order of the Commissioners of the Police in the Metropolis.'

When the order was issued, it was hoped by the stall-holders that it would not apply to Epsom—but their hopes were in vain, and their hastily devised memorial, taken to Sir James Graham, fell upon deaf ears for their spokesmen were curtly told that Sir James Graham was determined to suppress gambling on race-courses and his decision was irrevocable. The outcry against this supposedly pernicious decision was heard further afield than at Epsom, and at Ascot Lord Rosslyn announced that such a decree would inevitably lead to the diminution of the prize-money, with all the ramifications of owners finding racing more expensive. Proof that the lack of gaming-booths would affect racecourse attendances came the following day when the crowds who came to see the first day of the Derby meeting were very small by comparison to previous years. Not one of the accustomed games, from French Hazard to throwing for pincushions, was allowed and the half-completed and decorated booths illustrated the frustration and financial despair of the stall-holders.

In the evening further drama was caused by Lord George Bentinck producing the betting book of the jockey Sam Rogers and publicly announcing its contents as he stood on the steps of the Spread Eagle Inn at Epsom. Harry Hill, Lord George's commissioner who had warned him that Rogers had substantial bets on the Derby, may have acquired Rogers' book for him. 'It was a rich scene' commented a contemporary 'a motley crowd surrounded the aristocratic catechizer with grins of surprise or sly intelligence upon every countenance'. It was proposed that Pedley, John Gully's son-in-law, should call over the names, but his Lordship, with a whip under his arm and a gold pencil-case in his hand, commenced proceedings by tranquilly announcing, 'Gentlemen, I am going to call over my jockey, Samuel Rogers's book, and I will thank you to answer to your names and bets.'

20. Elis, winner of the 1836 St. Leger

21. Elis, with the horse-box which transported him from Good-wood to Doncaster

22. Plenipotentiary, Touchstone, Priam and Grey Momus

23. The Oaks 1845, won by the Duke of Richmond's Refraction

The first name called was that of Mr. John Gully, now committed to the Day's Danebury confederacy, who admitted that Rogers had backed both Ratan and The Ugly Buck with him. Lord George got little satisfaction from the onlookers, who in truth were afraid of him, but Rogers was discredited.

There had been scattered showers of rain over the weekend, but even so the Epsom course was bone hard, and the Stewards ordered tan to be distributed over it from start to finish before racing began on the Tuesday afternoon. There was very little betting on any of Tuesday's races, but the news that the Stewards had announced that Running Rein was qualified to run caused more money to be wagered on him. A further statement by Captain Rous, that although Running Rein was being allowed to run, this did not mean that the Steward's inquiries were at an end, did not deter the colts supporters.

After leaving the Spread Eagle Lord George Bentinck had gone to Crockford's home in Carlton Terrace and attempted to reassure both himself and Ratan's sick and ailing owner that all would be well on the morrow, but notwithstanding the fact that he had left instructions that Sam Rogers was to be locked up for the night in the same stable as Ratan with two lads on guard over them, he was worried about the outcome of the race. He would have been more worried if he had known that, despite all his security efforts, Ratan was nobbled during the night and the next morning 'his coat was standing like quills upon the fretful porcupine, his eyes dilated and he shivered like a man with the ague'. Crockford, too, was in distress. He had set his heart upon winning the Derby before he died, and he knew that Ratan was the best horse in the race. Years of experience of dealing with every type of gambler, from the aristocrat, who would lose an estate upon the turn of a card, to the sneak-thief who would cheat for the price of a drink, had given Crockford a nose for skull-duggery. Where Ratan was concerned he smelt villainy, but he was too tired and too ill to do anything about it. Gully also knew more than he cared to admit about Ratan and was confident that The Ugly Buck would win.

The roads from London to Epsom were crowded with vehicles of every description, barouches, phaetons, britzkas, tilburys and carts. Expensive park hacks, sturdy cobs and nags jostled each other in friendly rivalry as their riders exchanged pleasantries. Amongst the pedestrians, who cursed the dust thrown up by passing horsemen, were gypsies, tramps, shop boys, touts, ballad singers, beggars, prize fighters, ostlers and card-sharps. The number of carriages on the road made progress slow, and many race-goers took two hours to complete the last three miles of their journey from London. The heat and the dust made the assembled crowds thirsty, and the stall holders who had wisely turned their betting booths into drinking stalls did a prodigious trade, although they charged extortionate prices. Amongst the 'swells' who were determined to enjoy the outing no matter the outcome of the Derby were Guards officers, who lunched off plovers' eggs, pâté de foie gras, champagne, sherry cobbler and mint julip; nearby a group of butchers and their wives were stalwartly devouring cold crab, garlic sausage and bottled stout. A band of Italians with hurdy-gurdies played to the picnickers, and were rewarded with the remains of cold chicken and iced hock. Wanderers came back from the side-shows armed with their prizes, including jack-in-the-boxes, pincushions and gaily coloured wooden apples.

The police had trouble in clearing the course before the Derby, the first race of the day, was run. The 29 runners were:

Owner	Horse	Jockey
Mr. J. Day	The Ugly Buck	J. Day Jun.
Sir Gilbert Heathcote	Akbar	Chapple
Mr. Crockford	Ratan	Rogers
Mr. J. Day	Voltri	W. Day
Mr. J. Bowes	T'Auld Squire	Holmes
Sir Gilbert Heathcote	Campunero	Perren
Mr. A. Wood	Running Rein	Mann
Col. Peel	Orlando	Flatman
Col. Peel	Ionian	G. Edwards
Col. Anson	Bay Momus	Butler
Mr. Ford	Qui Tam	Robinson
Mr. J. Osborne	Mount Charles	Bumby
Mr. Ford	Phalaris	Whitehouse
Lord George Bentinck	Croton Oil	W. Howlett

Mr. Lichtwald	Leander	Bell
Mr. Hill	Beaumont	Calloway
Mr. Gratwicke	Needful	Cotton
Mr. Forth	The Ashtead Pet	Boyce
Mr. Herbert	colt by Elis	Sly
Lord Glasgow	colt by Velocipede	Hesseltine
Mr. Gregory	Loadstone	Darling
Lord Westminster	Lancet	Templeman
Mr. St. Paul	Telemachus	J. Marson
Mr. F. Ongley	King of the Gypsies	Marlow
Mr. M. Jones	British Tar	Jones
Mr. Cuthbert	Beaufront	J. Howlett
Lord Maidstone	Cockamaroo	Simpson
Mr. Dixon	Dick Thornton	Darling Jun.
Mr. Thornhill	Elemi	Chifney

S.P. 5–2 The Ugly Buck, 3–1 Ratan, 10–1 Running Rein, 14–1
Leander, 15–1 Ionian, 20–1 Orlando, Akbar, Qui Tam and Bay
Momus.

As the runners paraded before the race, Levi Goodman was on
tenterhooks. His daring fraud was now at its climax, and provided
that Running Rein won the Derby and those with whom he and
his confederates had wagered were prepared to settle their debts,
he would be a rich man. Two previously unconsidered facts,
however, were causing him great concern. The first was that in the
crowd surrounding Running Rein as he was saddled he had
noticed George Worley, Worley had come very close to the
horse, and Goodman had seen him shaking his head as though
in disbelief. It might be very untoward if at a later stage Worley
insisted that the horse he had seen at Epsom on Derby Day was
the four-year-old Maccabeus, who in 1842 had been kept at his
Northamptonshire farm.

The second unforseen circumstance was the appearance of a
horse named Croton Oil, sired by Physician and owned by Lord
George Bentinck. Croton Oil had not run as a two year old, but
he had won at the Epsom Spring Meeting. From Goodman's
viewpoint it was an unfortunate coincidence that Bentinck, of all
people, owned Croton Oil, for Croton Oil's dam and Maccabeus'
dam were the same mare! It was only a remote possibility that

99

the four-year-old Maccabeus and the three-year-old Croton Oil could be recognized as half-brothers, but the doubt lingered on.

At 3 o'clock, after two false starts, the runners were off. The start could not be seen from the grandstand, but as the horses appeared from behind the hill Leander was in the lead with Ratan and The Ugly Buck well placed just ahead of Akbar and Voltri. So much dust was kicked up by the leaders that the jockeys at the rear of the field found themselves blinded and choking for breath, and Cockamaroo and Dick Thornton gave up the struggle. Running Rein was soon tracking the leaders, just ahead of Ionian, Bay Momus and Orlando. At the end of the first half-mile Mann confidently sent Running Rein up to join Leander, who had already taken most of the runners off their feet by the pace he was setting. As the leaders reached the top of the hill Running Rein struck into the off hind leg of Leander, who crashed to the ground his leg smashed to smithereens above the fetlock. Running Rein was not impeded by this accident and stormed further ahead as the runners approached Tattenham Corner. He was several lengths clear at the turn into the straight, and as Akbar and The Ugly Buck weakened they were passed by Orlando, Ionian and Bay Momus. Ratan was exhausted and never at any stage of the race looked likely to be concerned in the finish, but for a moment the supporters of Colonel Peel's horses thought they might catch up and pass Running Rein. It was not to be, and Running Rein swept past the judge's box ahead of the gallant Orlando, with Ionian third and Bay Momus fourth. The stake to the winner was £4,250 and the judge, on the direction of the Stewards placed the first four—owing to the fact that a few weeks earlier the winner at Eglington Park had been disqualified and the judge had neglected to decree which horse was second.

Later in the afternoon Lord George Bentinck's Misdeal won the Epsom Stakes, and two other races were run before the crowds began to wend their way home. In the crush impatient coachmen caused carriages to over-turn with resultant broken bones for some of the occupants, but no one seemed in the least perturbed, for all thoughts were on the Derby result and the news that the owner of the second horse, Colonel Peel, intended to lodge an objection to the winner.

9

Colonel Peel, brother of Sir Robert Peel, Prime Minister in 1834 and again in 1841, was a friend and contemporary of the Duke of Richmond. When the Duke first owned racehorses he owned them in partnership with Jonathan Peel, and not until 1830 did Peel race in his own colours of 'purple, orange cap'. Two years later his horse Archibald won the 2,000 Guineas. A member of the Jockey Club, he was elected a Member of Parliament in 1826—the same year as Lord George Bentinck became the member for King's Lynn.

Like so many of his friends, he bet heavily, but more judiciously than the majority of them. He was a kind and generous man, and his behaviour towards the Earl of Glasgow over the 1844 Derby was typical of him. He had laid the Earl £10,000–£100 Ionian for the Derby thinking that his horse had no chance, for he believed his other contender Orlando to be far superior. As Derby Day approached he realized that the improving Ionian had more than an outside chance, and in consequence 'hedged' a greater part of his bet. On Derby day, so that the Earl might not think he had been cheated, Peel allowed him to give any instructions he wished to Ionian's jockey Edwards. Glasgow's instructions were equally typical 'let 'em fight it out'. Ionian's sire, Ion, owned by Colonel Peel, had run second in both the 1838 Derby and St. Leger before being retired as a stallion to the paddocks at Hampton Court, which for a time were leased by Peel and Charles Greville. In an era when there were so many undesirable rogues on the Turf, Colonel Peel stood out of complete integrity. It was to his further advantage as a man that he had a strong sense of humour, and an even stronger constitution.

In 1844 he had fifteen horses in training at Newmarket, including Orlando and Ionian. Orlando's two-year-old début had been at Ascot where, ridden by Nat Flatman, he had finished second, beaten three-quarters of a length by a filly of Mr. Wreford's trained by John Day. Amongst those horses who finished behind Orlando were horses owned by Colonel Anson, Lord Exeter, the Duke of Bedford and Lord George Bentinck. Orlando won his next two races, both at Newmarket. He won the Ham Stakes at Goodwood on the first day of the meeting, and won again on the Thursday, when he beat Leander. This was his last race of the 1843 season.

To what extent his objection to Running Rein was instigated by Lord George Bentinck is not of consequence. The rumours concerning Running Rein before the Derby, the manner in which he won the race, and the fact that so much money was at stake would have lead, inevitably, to some action from the Jockey Club; for in addition to Bentinck, Rous was aware of what was happening, and John Bowes wrote to his solicitor 'Running Rein belongs to a party of vagabonds who were at the bottom of Mr. Russells "Qui Tam" actions—they have won largely but I hope we shall be able to prove the horse four years old as he undoubtably is—'. Throughout the Saturday and Sunday following the Derby the only topic of conversation at Tattersalls concerned settlement of the Derby bets. Some suggested that all settlement should be postponed until the decision as to the winner of the Derby was legally agreed. Others were prepared to wager the outcome at 'evens' either horse. Sensibly Tattersalls committee sent out an edict on the Monday:

'At a meeting of the most influential subscribers to Tattersalls interested in the Derby and Oaks settlement, it was unanimously agreed that no possible impediment could exist to the settlement of all accounts on the Derby in which the names of Running Rein and Orlando do not occur, and that, therefore, the settling will take place this day as usual, with the above exceptions.'

The reference to The Oaks concerned the filly Julia, entered by Mr. Lichtwald, the owner of the Derby colt Leander, to whom

Lord Maidstone had objected on the grounds that he was a four year old. Colonel Anson and Squire Osbaldeston objected to Julia on the same grounds.

Another event which made the Derby settlement difficult was the death on Saturday 25th May of William Crockford, who having started life as a fishmonger, had bestrode gambling England like a colossus for a quarter of a century, and died an embittered man. In 1808, on the death of Mr. Panton, he bought his Newmarket house. Three years later he began racing in his 'white, red cap', and in 1819 his horse Sultan ran second in the Derby to the Duke of Portland's Tiresias. The following year Sultan won two Gold Cups and a thousand guineas match before being sold to Lord Exeter for a thousand guineas. For more than a decade Crockford's feud with John Gully, and the attempts of the two antagonists to defeat each other in their gambling activities on the Turf highlighted the extremes which vindictiveness could reach. Crockford died a rich man, reputed to be worth more than £350,000, but nevertheless there were those at Tattersalls who claimed that, by precedent, his death absolved the settlement of debts due to him. They were silenced when, two days after his death, his widow sent a letter to Mr. Tattersall:

'Sir—I trust the circumstances which cause me to address you will be a sufficient apology for so doing. Being ignorant of the custom in use at Tattersalls in situations parallel to the one I now find myself placed in, I consider it best for me at once to place in your hands the betting book of my deceased husband. You will perceive that in case Running Rein shall receive the stakes, there will be a loss of £604, and in case Orlando shall receive them, a loss of £724. I enclose you therefore a draft for the larger sum, and would wish you to apply this sum, together with the receipts from the several losers, to pay as far as may be the claims of the several winners. It is possible that, in a case of this sort, it is not customary to settle the book. Should it be so, I am not anxious to establish a precedent. With a deep sense of the trouble I am about to impose upon you, I have the honour to be, sir, yours most respectfully,

S. F. Crockford.
Carlton House Terrace. May 27. 1844.'

Mr. Tattersall also received a letter from the Stewards of the Jockey Club, signed by the Earl of Stradbroke and the Hon. George Byng, that every person indebted to the late Mr. Crockford on his Epsom account was bound to pay the amount due to the person deputed to settle the same. Notwithstanding the honesty of Mrs. Crockford, there were several who refused to settle their Derby and Oaks commitments.

It was announced in the Sheet Calendar that Colonel Peel, although not a party to the objection lodged against Running Rein prior to the Derby, had given notice to the stake-holders not to pay the Derby prize-money to Mr. Wood. and this notice had been endorsed by the Stewards. In the meantime the Stewards had received a letter from Mr. Gill, solicitor to Mr. Wood:

'Gentlemen: As solicitor for and on the part and behalf of Mr. Alexander Wood, the owner of Running Rein, I beg the favour of your appointing twelve o'clock on Monday next to proceed on the objection of the Hon. George Anson to the qualification of Running Rein and also to fix the hour of two o'clock of the same day to proceed on the evidence of disqualification to the same colt, to be offered on the part of Colonel Peel.

I am, gentlemen, your most obedient servant
Thomas Gill.
To Sir Gilbert Heathcote & Baron de Tessier.'

Mr. Gill delivered this letter personally to the Baron on the morning of The Oaks—two days after the Derby—and was requested to present himself to the Stewards at 4 o'clock the same afternoon, for an answer. At the appointed time, Baron de Tessier saw Mr. Gill and explained that Colonel Peel had left the racecourse, but that Colonel Anson expected to see him in London during the evening. The Baron, courteously regretting any inconvenience caused to Mr. Gill, proposed a further meeting at mid-day on the Saturday. There were further delays when Colonel Peel sent a letter stating that he was in consultation with his legal advisers and could not give a decision as to his intentions until Saturday evening. Finally a frustrated and ruffled Mr. Gill, who was joined by Mr. Wood himself, was informed that Colonel Peel offered to refer the matter to a barrister, to be selected by the

Lord Chief Justice of the Court of Queen's Bench, and also stated that he had begun an action against Messrs. Weatherby over the Derby prize-money. Mr. Wood, utterly disgruntled, refused to accept the Colonel's proposal, whereupon Baron de Tessier disclaimed any further action on the part of the Stewards, who were content to allow the affair to be adjudicated in a Court of Law.

A week later, with rumours rife about the outcome of the case, Lord George Bentinck wrote from London to his trainer at Goodwood:

'I am obliged to go to Ireland on business today, & think I shall hardly be back again before Wednesday or Thursday at earliest. I must leave you and Lord March to manage the horses entirely at Ascot . . . I won't go to William Sadler under any circumstances.'

Lord George went to Ireland to see Thomas Ferguson at Rossmore Lodge, for he was convinced that Ferguson could produce evidence which would incriminate Goodman. William Sadler, who Bentinck could not bring himself to see, was Goodman's trainer. The most obvious solution was that Bentinck hoped to see Ferguson's horse Goneaway alive. If he could see the horse and obtain corroborated evidence that Goneaway had impersonated Maccabeus at Epsom in the spring of 1843 this would go a long way towards ruining Goodman. Lord George had seen Goneaway when he had visited Ferguson previously at Rossmore Lodge, and years later commented on his visit in a letter to Lord Stanley, when he referred to Goneaway's impersonation of Maccabeus at the 1843 Epsom Spring Meeting:

'Goneaway had his picture taken as a foal & I had myself seen not only this picture of him but the horse himself only six months previous to his being disguised & disfigured after which I was purposely taken to see the horse & distinctly asked by William Sadler if he was Goneaway, where I very innocently declared I could readily swear he was not Goneaway!!!—horses change in colour & appearance so much as they get older that no description or registration could avail to identify a horse—I could instance a thousand cases.

Sir Charles Ibbotson was taken down to see Goneaway &

certified that he was Maccabeus deceived just as I was by his disguise.'

Thomas Coleman who trained horses at his Turf Hotel, St. Albans, for men such as John Gully and Prince Esterhazy was another to whom Lord George turned for information in his efforts to reach the truth regarding Running Rein, and in one letter he wrote to Coleman, he inquired about the movements of Maccabeus:

'Can the Ostler at Bryant's recollect a dirty, mean-looking little man, with light brown or sandy thin whiskers, with a bad knee, kicked by the horse he was leading up, stopping at the Red Lion to bait, on Saturday September 24, 1842 and asking his way either to Haines livery stables in Langham Place, or else to Mr. Goodman's stables in Foley Place? The colt he was leading up was a high courage, unbroke, or rather half broke bay, entire thoroughbred two year old colt with black legs, and not a white speck about him, and a long tail. The colt had also, at that time, a small scar scarcely healed up, on his near arm, just above the knee on the outside. ... The man & the colt were on their way to Smith's training stables at Epsom.'

Although in the days following the Epsom meeting there was incessant speculation as to the outcome of the Derby, the affair of Leander, who had been killed in the race, had not been forgotten. Leander had been full of running when Running Rein struck into him, and it is conceivable that, barring this accident, he would have gained first or second place with Mr. Wood's colt. If horses owned by Levi Goodman and the Lichtwald brothers had been victor and runner up then neither would have risked disqualification by objecting, no matter what arrangements were made between themselves behind the scenes. The Lichtwalds had been horse-dealers in Germany for many years and in 1835 Tattersalls had exported 33 horses to them. During Goodwood 1842 the brothers asked John Forth if they could send three horses to him to be broken and trained. The pedigree of these horses were written out on a piece of paper. Leander ran in a two-year-old race at Ascot in the summer of 1843 and won by two lengths. Shortly after Ascot the Lichtwalds went to Forth's stables at Michel Grove, near Arundel, and his son told them that there had been some rude remarks made at Ascot about the size and age of Leander. He was re-assured when he was told that the horse was correctly entered in the German Stud Book. At Goodwood Leander was second in a sweepstake to Colonel Peel's Orlando, and later on the same afternoon finished third in the Sussex Stakes, but did not race again during the 1843 season, although it had been intended to run him in the Criterion Stakes at Newmarket in the autumn. The day before the race he ran away with his stable lad, damaged his hock and was withdrawn.

In February 1844 Forth had two sick horses in his stable and called in a veterinary surgeon to attend them. Whilst the vet— confusingly a Mr. Wood from Arundel—was in his yard, Forth asked him to look into Leander's mouth, as he was a little doubtful as to the colt's age. Mr. Wood gave a certificate stating that Leander was a three year old, which, even if it did not allay Forth's suspicions, seemed ample justification for carrying on training Leander for the Derby with an easy conscience.

Leander did not run in the spring of 1844 and the Derby was his first race of the year. The events after Leander had been destroyed on the racecourse were astonishing. His lower jaw was sawn off by a Mr. James Mitchell of Worthing and his body hastily buried at Ashtead within hours of the Derby being over. Two nights later, after Colonel Anson's filly The Princess had won The Oaks, a boisterous party was held at John Scott's house at Leatherhead to celebrate the victory. Conversation turned to the objection to the filly, Julia, owned by the Lichtwalds, on the grounds that she was a four year old. The German brothers and their horses were abused, and in a moment of hilarious devilment, it was decided to go out into the night to exhume the body of the unfortunate Leander. The drunken grave-diggers must have been given a shock when they disinterred the body of the horse and discovered the lower jaw missing! One, at least, of the party was quick-witted enough to realize the implications and proposed that the remainder of Leander's head should be cut off. On Saturday morning the head was taken to Mr. Bartlett, a veterinary surgeon in Dorking who, after examining the upper jaw, pronounced that it was the head of a four year old. Meanwhile the elderly Mr. Forth not only admitted that the lower jaw was in his possession and that he had had it boiled to remove the flesh and preserve the teeth, but that he was taking it to London to the eminent veterinary surgeon, Mr. Field. To his annoyance, Mr. Field pronounced that it was the jaw of a four year old. In a furious temper, Mr. Forth went to Weatherbys office in Burlington Street where, by chance, he met Lord Stradbroke. He persisted in his belief that Leander was a three year old and the unfortunate Jockey Club Steward was compelled to listen to a tirade from the abusive and garrulous trainer. After hearing Mr. Forth out Lord Stradbroke pointed out the significance of the fact that the Lichtwald brothers had 'made themselves scarce' and had returned to Germany.

By this time the Stewards of the Jockey Club were fully aware of the enormity of the fraud of the Derby and were determined that such criminal affairs should not occur again. On Monday 17th June a meeting of the Club was held and resolutions passed concerning the age of horses and the disqualification of owners for wrongful description of their horses, thus confounding such foreigners as the Lichtwalds. In future no horse foaled out of the United Kingdom should be entered for any race where the Rules of the Jockey Club prevailed, unless the owner should, at the time of naming, produce to the person appointed to receive such nomination and leave with him a certificate from some racing club of the country where the horse was foaled, stating the age, pedigree and colour of the horse and the marks by which it was distinguished.

A week later a further meeting of the Jockey Club was held to discuss the Leander affair. Mr. Forth gave evidence and so did Mr. Bartlett, who insisted that the head brought to him at Dorking was the head of a four year old and that when the lower jaw, in the possession of Mr. Forth, was produced it fitted exactly into the upper jaw of Leander. Mr. Wood the Arundel vet, also gave evidence, but was thoroughly dissatisfied with the affair and wrote a letter to the *Morning Post* which ended:

'. . . As I am a plain countryman, quite unaccustomed to be questioned and cross questioned, but knowing my own business very well, I only want justice done to me.'

After hearing the evidence the Jockey Club members resolved

that the Lichtwalds should be for ever disqualified from racing under Jockey Club rules, and that the stakes won by Leander at Ascot in 1843 should be recovered and paid to the owner of the second horse. Lord George Bentinck was not present at this meeting, for he was in Ireland, but Colonel Peel attended, and so too did Charles Greville.

Much to Forth's indignation he was neither exonerated nor found guilty of any misdemeanour, but this did not deter him from continuing to rage and storm at all and sundry. He was in his dotage and became obsessed with the idea that the Jockey Club had a grudge against him, and wrote letters galore to the Press vindicating his reputation. He also showed the Press a letter he had received from the Lichtwalds from Berlin in which they claimed that Leander was unquestionably a three year old, no matter what anyone else said.

In yet another letter Forth dramatically announced:

'. . . I well know a certain party who, from a feeling of jealousy, have used their utmost endeavours and strained their every nerve to injure my character, and to crush me for many years past, but had they only remained quiet a short time longer it was my full determination that next Doncaster Races should have terminated my career on the Turf, for it has been a very long one, but now I publicly tell them I set them at defiance, and while by the blessings of Providence my health is allowed in me, will not suffer myself to be bullied off the Turf by them, relying as I do in full confidence, on the countenance and support of all honourable and just men.'

The implication is that the 'certain party' is the Jockey Club, who ended the affair in November 1844, by which time Forth was becoming a confounded nuisance. He bombarded the Jockey Club with protests and letters and, ultimately, it was agreed that a letter should be sent to him by Charles Weatherby:

'. . . The Jockey Club, therefore, passes no judgement against you in this matter, but as you are urgent for an expression of their opinion I am desired to say that they think you did not take the measures necessary to clear up the doubts which at one time existed in your own mind, and that a suspicion must therefore remain upon their minds that you were cognizant of the fact that the horse that ran for the Derby and the mare that ran for The

Oaks were more than three years old, both having been under your care for the latter part of the year 1842 until May 1844 . . .'

The opinions of members of the Jockey Club varied regarding the manner in which Sir Gilbert Heathcote and Baron de Tessier had managed the protest to Leander and Running Rein prior to the Derby. Lord George Bentinck led those who were not satisfied, and the letter written by the Baron agreeing to the Senior Stewards decree, that in future Epsom Races should be under the control and management of the Epsom Stewards conjointly with the Stewards of the Jockey Club, had done little to mollify them. At the Jockey Club meeting at Weatherbys on 15th June Charles Greville stated that he wished to call the attention of the Club to the fact that the Stewards of Epsom Races had refused to allow Colonel Peel's solicitor to see Mr. Wood's depositions, upon the strength of which they had allowed Running Rein to start for the Derby. Greville proposed that the Stewards of Epsom had acted wrongly, and that copies of the depositions should have been given to both Colonel Peel and other gentlemen who objected to the qualification of Running Rein. Of the 22 members present only Lord Exeter, Lord Rosslyn and Mr. Shelley opposed the motion, although some members had left the room before the division and Lord Albemarle declined to vote. Colonel Peel intimated that he had no fore-knowledge that Greville intended to introduce the resolution, copies of which Mr. Weatherby was ordered to send to the Epsom Stewards.

Baron de Tessier replied to Weatherby from Corpus Christi College, Oxford, on 18th June:

'. . . I have every wish, as one of the Stewards at Epsom, to defer to the opinions of the Jockey Club, but I fear I cannot in the present instance do so consistently with what is due to myself. The Declarations in my keeping were placed before the Stewards of Epsom as a basis on which to found a further and more extended investigation.

If the Gentlemen who objected to Running Rein, before and after the Race, had deemed it advisable to investigate the question of his qualifications before the Stewards of Epsom, as a preliminary to ulterior proceedings in a Court of Law if they deemed neccessary, they would have been in full possession of the matters contained in those Declarations and also would, so far as depended on the Stewards, have been able to examine in person the parties by whom the Declarations were made.

But it was thought more advisable to take the case at once into a Court of Law and so soon as that decision was formally stated to the Stewards of Epsom, they considered their functions had wholly ceased, and that they had no right to detain the Declarations, and certainly they had no wish to do so, save only with a view to justify their proceedings up to that time, if the propriety of such proceedings were called in question.

With this in view, solely, and for this purpose solely, I detained the Declarations with the consent of Mr. Wood's Attorney, and therefore I feel that without his consent I cannot with propriety make them public pending the present proceedings at Law.'

Nearly a year elapsed before a meeting of the Jockey Club was called at Baron de Tessier's request in consequence of Lord George Bentinck having made a charge against him of partial and unfair conduct as Steward of Epsom Races in the Running Rein affair and having objected, on that account, to his acting as referee in the inquiry as to the qualification of Iron Master to start for the 1845 Derby. Lord George made a detailed statement supporting his charge, and the Baron made an equally long explanation of his conduct. Both members then left the meeting, and their fellow members resolved:

'That in the investigation which took place as to the qualifications of Running Rein before the race at Epsom, the Baron de Tessier took an erroneous view of his duty as a Steward and ought not to have given a decision by which the horse was allowed to start upon the ex-parte statements of Mr. Wood and in the absence of the objectors to the qualification of Running Rein. That he was equally wrong in refusing to give to the solicitors of Colonel Peel, while the action was pending of Wood v Peel, copies of the affidavits on the strength of which his previous decisions had been made.

That this meeting acquits Baron de Tessier of any corrupt, or dishonest motive but censures him chargeable with great want of discretion in the exercise of his official functions.'

Rightly or wrongly, this resolution did not please the Baron who announced his resignation of the Stewardship of Epsom Races, and his withdrawal from the Jockey Club.

The summer meeting at Ascot was held 10 days after the Derby. Few of the horses which had competed at Epsom ran although The Princess won for Colonel Anson, Attila; his 1842 Derby winner, ran second for the Hunt Cup and the following day was started for the Gold Cup, in which race he broke down. Colonel Peel's Orlando walked over for two races and Ionian, having received a walk-over on the Tuesday, ran in the Gold Cup in which he finished third to Lord Albemarle's colt. The Royal meeting was marred by an incident in the New Stakes for two year olds. Mr. F. Herbert's Bloodstone led from start to finish, cantering in some six lengths ahead of his nearest rival. On returning to scale, John Day, who had ridden Old England the 2–1 favourite who had finished second, promptly objected to Bloodstone on three counts. Firstly that Bloodstone was a three year old, secondly that his owner or Mr. Newman (the trainer) was in arrears of stakes with a member of the Jockey Club, and thirdly that Bloodstone's pedigree was wrongly stated. To make these counts even more scurrilous, the rumour soon got round that Mr. Herbert and Mr. Newman had given Bell, Bloodstone's jockey, instructions not to win, but that Bell, out of spite, disregarded the orders! This rumour was to an extent substantiated by the fact that Bloodstone was not quoted in the betting.

The Ascot Stewards, unlike Baron de Tessier and Sir Gilbert Heathcote at Epsom, acted with alacrity. Within 24 hours, Mr. Field had been brought down from London to examine Bloodstone, and another veterinary surgeon, Mr. Parry from Reading, was asked for a second opinion. Mr. Field, who had recently pronounced the jaw and head of the decapitated Leander to be that of a four year old, did not hesitate in declaring that Bloodstone was a three year old. Mr. Parry confirmed this opinion and, the Stewards awarded the race to Old England.

Except that Mr. Herbert brought an action, which he lost, against Weatherbys for the recovery of the stake, the matter ended there, unlike the case of Wood v Peel which was heard in the Court of Exchequer on Tuesday 2nd July, when Mr. Wood, owner of Running Rein, sued Colonel Peel for the return of the Derby stakes.

IO

During the month of June the horse known as Running Rein who had won the Derby was stabled at Smith's at Epsom. So also was the three year old whom Maccabeus had impersonated. Mr. Wood, obviously distressed by the possibility of his Derby winner being disqualified, was at a loss as to what action to take. He backed horses only in a modest way, and for him the glory of his Derby triumph was ample honour—but it was an honour he was determined to keep, if it was possible. He was afraid of no man and he refused to be brow-beaten. His reasons for bringing the lawsuit were explained in a letter written by his solicitor and published in Bell's *Life*:

'Mr. Wood's beneficial interest in the stake being but small, he endeavoured to avoid a lawsuit, and to have the dispute decided by the Stewards: but the instant that Colonel Peel commenced the action, in which the issue Wood v Peel was framed, Mr. Wood refused in my presence, and with my advice as his solicitor, to litigate a matter in which he had so little interest, but being positively assured, and believing that the horse was Running Rein, he, upon receiving a bond of indemnity, permitted those who had greater interest than himself in the stakes, to use his name for the purpose of trying the question, and to employ their own Attorney, the use of Mr. Wood's name being necessary for the purpose . . .'

Behind the scenes, the protagonists were Levi Goodman and Lord George Bentinck. Goodman was not likely to be the loser financially if the Derby was awarded to Orlando because he had ample opportunity, since the Derby, to wager at Tattersalls on

Orlando ultimately being declared the winner, and to most of his bets he had managed to get even money. His loss, however, would still be disastrous, for not only would he not collect his winning bets on Running Rein, but infinitely worse he would be utterly discredited, and warned off the Turf. When he knew that a lawsuit had been put down for hearing, he realized that he had little time in which to act. Whatever charges of villainy were laid against him, no one could accuse him of being either unintelligent or a fool, although, like so many other criminals, his contempt for the authority of 'right and might' proved his downfall. He appreciated that once the question of Running Rein's identity was questioned in a Court of Law, a host of witnesses would be called, particularly those connected with the colt he had bought from Sir Charles Ibbotson. He knew that in Lord George Bentinck he had an adversary, ruthless, energetic and merciless, who was out to discredit him, not only to rid the Turf of a scoundrel but also for the personal prestige which would thus be gained. He knew too that Bentinck had been to Ireland since the Derby and had seen Ferguson, the owner of Goneaway, who was virtually guaranteed to have given Bentinck the information he needed.

It was clear that the four-year-old Maccabeus, who had impersonated Running Rein, must disappear since he foresaw that the crux of the lawsuit would be yet another examination of Running Rein. Witnesses could perjure themselves until blue in the face—and probably would—but the Judge would decide on his summing up to the jury by reference to the age of Running Rein. If an examination of Running Rein was required, very well, Judge, jury, veterinary surgeons and witnesses could see the colt by The Saddler out of Mab, who genuinely was a three year old. After all, he had cleverly switched the two-year-old Running Rein for the three-year-old Maccabeus at Newmarket the previous autumn. Why should he not hood-wink everyone again? With the four year old out of the way and the three year old produced as evidence, how could anyone defeat him? Six weeks after the Derby, how could it be proved that his three year old had not run at Epsom on Derby Day, when the two horses looked alike? Buoyed up by these thoughts, Levi Goodman faced the forthcoming trial with much more confidence than was deserved. Maccabeus, alias Running Rein, was mysteriously and secretly taken away from Smith's stables, and not heard of again until long after the trial was over. It seemed to Goodman that he had played his hand so well that it was impossible for anyone to defeat it.

But Lord George Bentinck had every intention of trumping Goodman's cards, even if he had to revoke to do so. His informers had made it quite clear to him years ago that Levi Goodman was a villain. He was convinced that Goodman had outwitted him the previous autumn when the Newmarket Stewards had over-ruled the objection to Running Rein, and he had sworn revenge. Nothing would stop him from finally ruining Goodman, now that the Derby fraud was to be brought to light in the Law Courts. He had been to Ireland and interviewed Ferguson at Rossmore Lodge. Ferguson had been reluctant to see him and had pretended to be ill, but he had demanded a hearing and now knew all about the part Goneaway had played in impersonating Maccabeus. He had evidence too, from a hairdresser, Rossi, that Goodman had bought a dye with which to make Goneaway look more like Maccabeus before he ran at the Epsom Spring Meeting of 1843. The more he considered every aspect of the case, the more hours and days he spent in his counsel's chambers going over the minutest detail, the more convinced he became that Goodman could not avoid his just deserts.

Obviously as his counsel pointed out, the Judge would require the Derby winner to be produced and that would hoist Goodman with his own petard. In a moment of horror Bentinck suddenly saw the loophole through which Goodman could escape. He had too high a regard for Goodman's criminal intelligence to doubt that he might have overlooked such a loophole. The realization that all his efforts might be in vain made him angry beyond the bounds of reason. The loophole, of course, was the disappearance of the four year old who had masqueraded as Running Rein. How could a judge and jury find in favour of the defendant, Colonel Peel, if Mr. Wood produced the genuine three-year-old Running Rein from Smith's Epsom stables, after Goodman had spirited the four year old away. Wood, honest and abounding in integrity, was a mere pawn in the game and needed scant consideration. But if his enemy, Goodman, successfully got rid of Maccabeus, then there was a distinct possibility that the lawsuit would be decided in Wood's favour. His only hope was to be able to prove that the three-year-old Running Rein had not run at Epsom on Derby Day, but no matter how many witnesses he produced, a jury might not accept their evidence. What other hope had he? As he too, like Goodman, tossed and turned seeking for a solution, a scheme audacious, possibly criminal, certainly unorthodox, came to him. If he put it into practice and it succeeded, Goodman, without the slightest doubt, would be utterly ruined. If it failed, it would rebound upon him to the disgrace of not only himself, but also of the Jockey Club and his family. The scheme was to organize the stealing of the three-year-old Running Rein, so that when the judge demanded the examination of the Derby winner, no horse could be produced, for he presumed Goodman would not dare to produce the four year old.

Whether or not Bentinck was responsible for the secret disappearance of the three-year-old Running Rein must be open to conjecture and doubt; but there is one certainty—when the case was heard in the Court of Exchequer there was no horse known as Running Rein in Smith's stable at Epsom, for both the four year old and the three year old had vanished.

II

The case of Wood v Peel was heard before Baron Alderson and a jury on Monday 1st July 1844 at the Court of Exchequer at Westminster. The court was crowded to capacity, and amongst the well-known racing personalities present were Lord Stradbroke, Charles Greville, Captain Rous and Lord George Bentinck. To the racing world it was eminently satisfactory that Baron Alderson was to judge the case, for he was recognized as one of the few judges who understood and enjoyed racing. Educated at Charterhouse and Caius College, Cambridge, he was declared a Senior Wrangler in January 1809 at the age of twenty-one, and shortly afterwards was elected to a Fellowship, before going to London to read law, where he had been entered at the Inner Temple. Called to the Bar in 1811 he joined the Northern circuit and Yorkshire sessions, and it was whilst in Yorkshire that he frequently visited the trainer John Scott at Malton. But if Alderson was a learned and distinguished Judge, the leading barristers on both sides were equally distinguished, and it was their appearance which gave the case an even greater aura of importance. Wood's solicitor had briefed Mr. Alexander Cockburn, who in future years was to prosecute the infamous poisoner William Palmer, and later become Lord Chief Justice of England. Leading for Colonel Peel was the newly knighted Sir Frederick Thesiger, the Solicitor General, who years later was created Baron Chelmsford. He knew Lord George Bentinck, and it was largely through Lord George's influence that he stood as Member of Parliament for Newark in 1840.

No sooner had Baron Alderson taken his place, than Mr.

Cockburn rose and, to everyone's surprise, requested that all witnesses on both sides should withdraw. Immediately Sir Frederick Thesiger, demanded whether or not such a request would include Lord George Bentinck, and Mr. Cockburn stated that it must include Lord George, whom he considered to be the real defendant in the case, even though he had been subpoenaed by Mr. Wood and not by Colonel Peel. Baron Alderson commented that he could see no reason why Mr. Cockburn wished to exclude his own witnesses when the Solicitor General was prepared for them to remain in Court. In accepting the Judge's comment Mr. Cockburn explained that he thought that Lord George Bentinck would be a hostile witness, but that he would not pursue this matter any further. He wished to point out, however, that it seemed wrong that Lord George had taken his seat between the counsel for the plaintiff and the defendant and he wished that he would go and sit elsewhere.

In his opening address to the jury Mr. Cockburn made it clear that the issue was a question of identity, and that he was confident that he could prove to them that Running Rein was a three year old when he won the Derby, and he would call witnesses to substantiate his submissions. One witness he would not call would be Mr. John King, a training groom from Malton, who had recently entered the employment of Lord George Bentinck. He went on to repeat categorically that it was not Colonel Peel who was deeply interested in the result, but rather Lord George Bentinck.

Mr. Cockburn next proceeded to outline Running Rein's history up to the time of the objection lodged against him at Newmarket in the autumn of 1843. In *The Times* the next morning, he was quoted as continuing:

'A competent authority had decided that the horse was as young as he was stated to be by Mr. Goodman, and the plaintiff (Mr. Wood) bought him, in fact with all his engagements. Than this nothing could be more open, and it was very hard upon the plaintiff now to revive that old objection, and to submit it to another tribunal. It might be urged today that Mr. Goodman was a man of no character on the Turf. So he might be, but that was no reason why the plaintiff should be included in the consequences. Talk of morality! Why, where was the morality of certain noble lords and others, who, knowing the objection to this horse, yet betted largely against him, content to take the money if they won, but determined to revive the protest and refuse to pay if they were unsuccessful. That was the honour of some members of the Turf, whom, if they should venture to place themselves in the witness-box, he promised to turn inside out on that point in five minutes, and expose their boasted honour to the world for what it was really worth. These were the parties who were deeply interested in this case. They had betted deeply against the horse, and they had betted deeply against the plaintiff's chance of success in the case. Was that a way to support the honour of the Turf? He imagined not. Such an inquiry as this ought never to have been brought before the present tribunal. Deeply as he venerated the sacred character of the British Bench, and a British jury, he could not but think that such a tribunal was desecrated by being made the arbiters of such a cause as this. It was very desirable that the Jockey Club should have been selected as the Judges on such an occasion, for that was an atmosphere far better suited to it than the present.'

The first witness called by Mr. Cockburn was Thomas Lofthouse who gave evidence concerning the birth of the colt by The Saddler out of Mab, born at Malton in May 1841. He was followed into the witness-box by John Kitchen who as a seventeen year old had cared for him at Malton. Kitchen had been unemployed for the month since the Derby, and had been living with a Mr. Glenn, a Regent Street biscuitmaker who was known to be of dubious reputation.

Henry Stebbings was next into the witness-box. His answers were evasive and he was not prepared to swear that the horse he had seen at Newmarket in October 1843 was the colt he had bought for Levi Goodman.

After he stepped down, Baron Alderson asked whether or not the horse was available, to which the Solicitor General replied that, although an order signed by the Judge for the inspection of the horse had been given, permission had been refused to see Running Rein. It was the first indication to those present at the Court of Exchequer that there might be a mystery about the whereabouts of the horse, and the judge himself showed signs of surprise, by commenting:

'There may be good reasons for that refusal, but it will only be over-looked by some production of the horse now. I sit here as a court of conscience, and I feel—and I am sure the jury feel too—that an examination and production of this horse are indispensable. After this notice I shall expect to see the horse myself, and I should like to look at his mouth myself.'

The next witnesses called were Robert Spanlon, who was in the service of Mr. King at Malton, James Stebbings and Daniel White, who had been responsible for taking the colt by The Saddler out of Mab from one stable to another after his arrival in London. All of them corroborated the movements of the colt brought from Yorkshire, as did William Bean, Drewett, George Hitchcock, who broke the colts at Epsom and William Smith the trainer. As the Judge and jury anticipated, Mr. Cockburn was attempting to build up, by a massive amount of detailed, and at times confused, evidence, the life history of the colt by The Saddler out of Mab, foaled in Yorkshire. Two factors made his task difficult. The first was that none of the witnesses put by him into the box seemed prepossessing, and none of them seemed convincing. Their clothes were untidy and their evidence, at times, almost inaudible. Bean was discredited in cross-examination, and after his replying to one question 'I have no recollection of the circumstances,' Baron Alderson caused laughter by commenting, 'May I venture to ask you if you have ever committed a murder? Perhaps you have no recollection of that'. The second factor causing Cockburn difficulty was the bewildering number of times that the horse had switched stables, and apparently always at a time when there were other horses being brought to and from the stables. If nothing else, this must have appeared suspicious to the jury.

It was at this stage that the spectators were given their second inkling that there was a mystery about the whereabouts of Running Rein for William Smith, the Epsom trainer, told the court that five days previously the horse had been taken away from his stables. He claimed that he had received a verbal order from Mr. Wood to give the horse to a Mr. Ignatius Coyle, a tall man with a red face, and added that he had begged Mr. Wood to take the horse out of his possession for he was getting afraid, as there were so many people around the stables at every hour of the day and night. Baron Alderson interrupted:

'And so, in your fear, you gave up this horse to a man who came to claim it in Mr. Wood's name, without any written order from Mr. Wood?'

Witness—'I had seen him go to Mr. Wood's my Lord, the night before and'. . .

Mr. Baron Alderson (with warmth)—'No, now I see the whole drift of it. This was the very day before my order reached the place, which order was contemptuously disobeyed, I say it was treating this Court most contemptuously and I'll take care that the parties shall hear of it again next term.'

Witness—'Your Lordship's order was read to me and I said, if they required it I would go to Mr. Wood's, and get his authority to give up the horse.'

Mr. Baron Alderson—'And you said this, Sir, at the very time when you knew that the horse had been taken away, and you had no idea where. Why did you not say the horse was not there, Sir?'

Witness—'I was not asked the question, my Lord.'

Mr. Baron Alderson—'I don't believe you, Sir. It was sent away in anticipation of my order, and was a gross contempt of Court, for which you will have to answer next term.'

Mr. Cockburn—'There will be time enough, my Lord, to discuss that point when' . . .

Mr. Baron Alderson—'Oh, yes; no doubt there will be time enough for it. It appears to me that justice demands the production of this horse, for the inspection of the jury and myself.'

Mr. Cockburn—'There will not be the slightest objection, my Lord, to produce the horse for the inspection of your Lordship and the jury.'

Mr. Baron Alderson—'Then give me leave to say, that I shall show it to anybody I please. The truth is always best arrived at by openness and frankness. If the mouth be a fallible criterion, then let its fallacy be shown at once; and let the jury be told by me that they are to treat it accordingly. This will not be done by concealing the truth; justice can never be served by that means.'

Mr. James—'The witnesses, my Lord, have distinctly proved the identity.'

Mr. Baron Alderson—'Either the mark in the mouth is, or is not, a fallible criterion. Let us have the advantage of seeing it and testing it fairly.'

In further examination by Mr. Cockburn, William Smith claimed that he knew nothing about the order signed by Baron Alderson for the production of the horse until it was brought personally to him—by none other than Lord George Bentinck himself. When Lord George was told that the horse he had come to collect, with the authority of the law to support him, had already disappeared he was aghast—or pretended to be. Many years later Ignatius Coyle claimed that he had spirited Running Rein away from Smith's stable under the nose of everyone by riding his own hack into the stable yard, quickly saddling Running Rein and riding him out of the yard without anyone noticing!

Only one more witness was called by plaintiff's counsel, Baron de Tessier, who did little more than state the manner in which he and Sir Gilbert Heathcote had dealt with the protest lodged by Lord George Bentinck against Running Rein before the Derby. Significantly, from his own point-of-view, he also made the comment 'I have taken some interest in horse-racing, but I have had quite enough of it'.

Sir Frederick Thesiger, opening the case for the defendant, Colonel Peel, decried the attack made by Mr. Cockburn upon Lord George Bentinck who, in his opinion, had acted throughout in a manner which should be applauded and not condemned for Bentinck 'was desirous that frauds such as were here imputed, and which he was fully prepared to prove, should be annihilated'. The Solicitor General, after explaining to the jury that the defendant was at a disadvantage because 'in this court he is tied by strict legal evidence, whilst out of it he would have been enabled to introduce facts of the most important nature which now must be omitted', pointed out why Mr. Cockburn had not called Levi Goodman as a witness. In his opinion Goodman was the one man who knew everything about the entire affair, but if he was put into the box and could therefore have been cross-examined, he would have been asked some very awkward questions. Of those who had been called by the plaintiff, none proved with any certainty that the horse passed from hand to hand and stable to stable was always the same and the evidence of a man of the character of William Bean was worthless.

The Solicitor General then turned the attention of the jury to the horse Maccabeus, bred by Sir Charles Ibbotson. Unfortunately from the defendant's point of view, the man who had brought Maccabeus from Worley's farm to London in September 1842 had vanished, and despite every effort to trace him he could not be found. If he had been found he could have, at once, been able to say whether or nor the horse he took to London and the Running Rein who won the Derby were the same horse.

The Solicitor General continued to speak for another hour, outlining the career of Maccabeus and the part that Thomas Ferguson of Rossmore Lodge had played in the substitution of Goneaway for Maccabeus, before ending his peroration by expressing a hope that he would make out such a case as would command a case for the defendant, and so by that verdict the jury would read a salutary lesson to men such as Goodman and thereby clear the Turf of every man of similar character, to the regeneration of horseracing, which was threatened with destruction in consequence of the recent exposures.

After Sir Frederick Thesiger sat down, Lord Stradbroke and Mr. Charles Weatherby were called, merely to give evidence of a technical nature as to entries for races. It was past 7 o'clock and everyone had been subjected to an exhausting day. Both Mr. Cockburn and the Solicitor General had outlined and detailed their client's cases with immense skill, and only one item of supreme importance remained unanswered—where was the horse?

London on the morning of Tuesday 2nd July was drenched by torrential rain, and those who arrived by foot at the court for the second day of the case were soaked. As the barristers and lawyers took their places a consultation was held between Baron de Tessier, Colonel Peel and Lord George Bentinck. A moment later they were joined by Mr. Wood. All eyes were turned towards the group, and whispered guesses as to the subject of the discussion grew in volume when it was seen that Wood had produced a piece of paper and shown it to Colonel Peel who, after glancing at it, shook his head and returned to his seat. Further conjecture was prevented by the arrival of the Judge.

Mr. Cockburn began on a diffident note by admitting that both he and his client Mr. Wood felt it difficult to proceed without the production of Running Rein. After the court was adjourned the previous evening, Mr. Wood had gone first to Smith's stables at Epsom and then to Goodman's at Sutton but, much to his consternation and embarrassment, Running Rein was at neither place. The Judge interposed that if the horse had been stolen, he would try the parties who had removed him at the Central Criminal Court and have them transported for the felony. The case continued with the examination by the Solicitor General, of Mr. George Worley, at whose farm the Gladiator colt, Maccabeus, had been kept as a yearling. Mr. Worley had been at Epsom on Derby Day 1844 and had no hesitation in stating that the horse he saw parading in the paddock before the Derby was the horse who had been at his farm two years earlier, and no amount of subsequent interrogation by Mr. Cockburn altered his belief.

At this moment, after a hurried consultation with Mr. Wood, Mr. Cockburn admitted defeat. Addressing the Judge he explained that, prior to the hearing of the case that morning, Mr. Wood had handed a letter to Colonel Peel stating that he was satisfied that there was a fraud concerning his horse, and he wished to withdraw from the case. In consequence he, Mr. Cockburn, was willing to submit to a verdict for the defendant; although he could not do so without expressing, on behalf of Mr. Wood, the assertion that he had not had any part in the fraud, of which he had in fact been the victim. He trusted, therefore that it would be realized that he was an honourable man. Mr. Cockburn then continued:

'And now, my Lord, perhaps I may be allowed to allude to another circumstance. It may be in your Lordship's recollection, that in my address to the jury, I had occasion to allude to Lord George Bentinck, and to speak of his connexion with this case in very strong terms. My Lord, I last night received a communication from his Lordship, couched, I must say, in the most courteous terms, and by no means complaining of any improper exercise of my professional privileges yesterday, but of my having abstained from putting him into the box, after I had perused my instructions, and spoken of his conduct as I did, so that he had been deprived of the opportunity of refuting the charges I had brought against him, while I had abstained from attempting to prove them. My Lord, I do not blame his Lordship for this course, but I may perhaps be allowed to say, that my instructions on the subject were of the fullest, amplest, and most precise character. I was instructed that Lord George Bentinck had interfered and unduly exerted himself in getting up this case; that he had taken some of the witnesses to his own residence, Harcourt House, where he had tampered with them. I was instructed that in one case he had expressly given money to a witness, and in another that he had offered indirectly pecuniary assistance to another. All this, I was instructed, would be borne out by evidence; but though Lord George Bentinck does not know it, it is well known both to your Lordship and to the learned counsel for the defence, that I could not arrive at proof of these facts if they were truly stated to me by putting his Lordship into the box, or by asking any questions of my own witnesses relative to his supposed interference, as he was not a party to the cause. I fully expected to be able to do so, as I stated, on the cross-examination of those persons to whom I alluded; and I thought it my duty towards my learned friends and to his Lordship openly and boldly to give expression to my instructions in my opening speech; so that it should not be said that I had waited for my reply, when no answer could be given, to make an attack upon that nobleman's character. That was my reason for the course I then pursued, and I trust that I shall receive credit for having confined myself strictly to the discharge of my professional duty. I have thought it right to enter into this explanation, in order that, as the case has abruptly terminated, his Lordship may take such a course as he may be advised to set himself right, either by denying the truth of the charges, or explaining them in any other way, by himself or by his friends.' Mr. Baron Alderson commented 'I am sure that no one can say that you were not justified in making observations upon the conduct of Lord George Bentinck'. The letter from Lord George to which Mr. Cockburn referred was:

'Harcourt House, July 1, 1844
Monday night.

Sir—I am too fully cognizant of your duty as well as privilege as a counsel, and much too highly appreciate the value and usefulness of such a privilege, for a moment to question the propriety of the remarks which you felt it right, I doubt not, in obedience to your instructions, to pass upon my conduct this morning.

I am quite aware that an honest counsel is professionally bound to assume as true all that is stated in his brief, and would betray his trust if he were to spare the feelings of any one against whose integrity and uprightness he either had, or might be misled by his instructions to believe he had, any facts, proofs, or evidence to adduce.

Conceiving the latter to be your position this morning, I admired the manliness and honesty with which you made your attack, though I myself was the victim of it, perfectly content on my own account patiently to abide my time, when I confidently anticipated you would put me into the witness-box, and thereby at once prove your words to be true, or convince yourself and all the world besides, that grave charges were never made with less foundation against mortal man, than those you hurled at me.

As in duty bound, I was in court under your client's subpoena, and had brought with me all the documents in my power to bring, in faithful and honest obedience to the wide scope of your duce tecum subpoena: bound by my oath, I should have had no choice to answer freely every question you had thought proper to put to me; but more than that, I pledge you my word as a man of honour and as a gentleman, that if you had put me in the witness-box, or will still do so, where your instructions or your own acuteness had fallen, or may fall, short in directing your examination, I would have freely and frankly supply, the want, and will fully disclose every act of mine connected with this transaction. Having said this much, I appeal to you, not in the way of a threat (for I have none to make, and have none in thought or reservation) but I, as a supplicant, appeal to you as a man of honour, honesty and truth, to afford me that redress to which I have pointed, without which your opening speech cannot be justified.'

In summing up the lawsuit Baron Alderson said:

'Now, Gentlemen of the Jury, you have only to return a verdict for the defendant, the plaintiff as you have heard, declining to contest the question any further. There is, therefore, an end to the case, but before we part, I might be allowed to say that it has produced great regret and disgust in my mind. It has disclosed a wretched fraud, and has shown noblemen and gentlemen of rank associating and betting with men of low rank and infinitely below them in society. In so doing they have found themselves cheated and made the dupes of the grossest frauds. They may depend upon it that it will always be so when gentlemen associate and bet with blackguards.'

So ended the Wood v Peel case. Lord George Bentinck left London for Winchester that night and the following day saw his four-year-old colt Fisticuff win a sweepstake at the local race-meeting. Goodman, discredited, had fled for France, not only to escape the law but also his creditors.

Two days later there appeared a notice in *The Times*:

'The noblemen and gentlemen of the Jockey Club, several proprietors of race-horses and others interested in the honour and prosperity of the Turf intend to present Lord George Bentinck with a piece of plate to mark their sense of the immense service he has rendered to the racing community by detecting and defeating the attempt at fraud exposed in the late trial in the Court of Exchequer. The subscription is to be confined to £25 and from the number of names already down at Messrs Weatherbys, comprising some of the highest on the Turf, it will no doubt be a very large one.'

Before the Newmarket Houghton meeting it had reached £2,000.

At a meeting of the Jockey Club on Saturday 6th July a resolution was passed:

'That the thanks of the Jockey Club are eminently due and are hereby offered to Lord George Bentinck for the energy, perseverance and skill which he has displayed in detecting, exposing and defeating the atrocious frauds which have been brought to light during the recent trial respecting the Derby stakes.'

At the same meeting it was agreed that, as from 1845, an additional £2 per annum be paid by every member of the Jockey Club to form a fund for the prosecution of parties guilty of fraud in horse racing.

When replying to the Jockey Club, Lord George wrote to them through Charles Weatherby:

'I request that you will signify to the Stewards and other members of the Jockey Club the deep sense I entertain of their partiality and favour in bestowing upon me the unanimous vote of their thanks for the exposure of a great national fraud in the accomplishment of which so many fellow labourers have toiled with no less zeal and far more ability than I.'

A week after the end of the lawsuit, it was again rumoured that the four-year-old Maccabeus was dead, but the rumour was not confirmed, and was later proved to be false. The whereabouts of the three-year-old Running Rein was never discovered. At Tattersalls the settling of the Epsom accounts was resumed, but the settling proved very unsatisfactory, for several heavy losers appeared neither in person nor by proxy. *The Times* fired a broadside:

'The absence of 2 or 3 of these persons is goodnaturedly attributed to ignorance of the time fixed for settling although made public in all the Daily papers on Friday last & copied into most of the provincial & weekly journals. This plea cannot therefore be allowed and for their neglect to make any provision for the settlement no excuse whatever can be made. It is in the highest degree reprehensible. Of 2 other cases no hopes whatsoever are entertained. It was well known long ago that they would be "wanted" if Orlando won and no one is in the least surprised at their absence. These deficiencies and the state of abeyance in which the late Mr. Crockford's book remains, has a most disheartening influence on the settlement, all the accounts having been more or less disarranged, and several parties, good winners on the race, obliged in consequence to leave the Room considerably out of pocket. The only way to prevent this very unusual consequence of extravagant and indiscriminate "Bookmaking" is without regard to rank or station, to adopt the "blackboard", and post not only actual defaulters, but all who fail to attend or make arrangements for paying and receiving on the regular settling day.'

24. Lord George Bentinck.
Sketch from the *Illustrated
London News*, 1848

25. Welbeck Estate, the
water meadow where Lord
George Bentinck died

26. Welbeck Abbey

27. Plan of Epsom Race-course

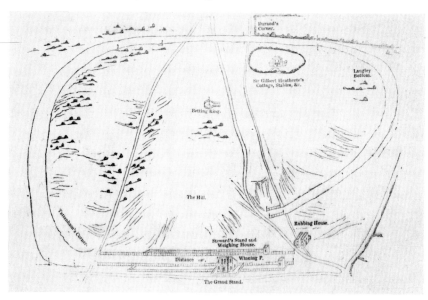

12

Throughout the year 1844 Lord George continued his efforts to improve the efficiency of the administration of race meetings. Amongst his reforms was his insistence that jockeys were attired in silk, velvet or satin colours and top-boots and breeches. The leading professional jockeys of the era rode with skill and verve, but amateur riders deservedly came in for considerable ridicule, summed up in a contemporary poem:—

'A vast assemblage this, where boys from school
In jockey's garbs first come to play the fool;
Oxonian thick-heads, eminently dense,
Who yearly meet to prove their want of sense,
And give their steeds that whip-cord—truant elves!
Which wiser nature destined for themselves
And now where every block-head bends his back,
Like Puss resisting Pompey's rough attack,
To spur the sides of some ill-fated track;
Where giant ponies, Lilliputian peers,—
Some scarcely breeched, and some advanced in years,
Militia bucks, and Cornets of Dragoons,
Like showmen habited, or stage buffoons
With wasted carcasses their rips bestride,
And puff, perspire, and pant and think they ride.'

Bentinck rode for the last time in public at the Goodwood meeting in July, when he was beaten a neck on his own horse Captain Cook. The race was over the Cup course and he was defeated by Lord Maidstone on Larrie McHale who was giving him seven pounds. A month after the Goodwood meeting the

St. Leger was won by Foigh-a-Ballagh, trained by John Forth. There had been doubts expressed at Tattersalls as to the manner in which he had been scratched from the Derby at the eleventh hour, and after his St. Leger victory aspersions were cast upon his age. He had been bred in Ireland and had been sold to his owner Mr. Irwin in a batch of eight horses for a total price of two thousand guineas. Subsequently Foigh-a-Ballagh won the Grand Duke Michael stakes and the Cesarewitch, and then finished second in the Cambridgeshire—a remarkable achievement whatever his age.

The bitterly cold winter of 1844–45 prevented many trainers from exercising their horses until the spring. At Goodwood the foresight of Lord George Bentinck enabled his 36 horses and those of the Duke of Richmond to be cantered on the straw-covered exercise grounds which were sheltered by plantations of trees, and on the nearby Halnaker gallop, which had been laid out in one of the woods of the park. This gallop, enclosed by beech trees, stretched for 1½ miles from Halnaker to the crest of the hill on the road leading from the racecourse to Petworth. On some of the gallops as much as six inches of mould had been laid at Lord George's instruction, which enabled the horses to be given fast work despite the snow and frost. Bentinck was in his element and felt that he personally had defeated the weather when other lesser mortals had failed to do so.

Hundreds were 'put in his pocket' when at the Northampton and Pytchley Hunt meeting at the end of March his horses won three races, and he gambled heavily on all of them. As a subterfuge he ran his three-year-old colt, Clumsy, in the opening race of the meeting, knowing that the colt had little chance of success, but nevertheless telling all and sundry that he thought that Clumsy would win. After Clumsy had been decisively beaten, few besides Lord George realized that his horses were fit, and in consequence he managed to get better odds on his three winners, the last of whom was John O'Gaunt, who defeated Squire Osbaldeston's filly Sorella, the 2–1 on favourite. Lord George thought this a major triumph and was far more delighted with the fact that he had beaten his old adversary than that his horse had vanquished Sorella, the winner of the 1844 One Thousand Guineas. The subsequent week Discord, fresh from his victory in the Great Northamptonshire Stakes, won two more races at Croxton Park. It seemed that Lord George's horses were invincible, but the task of keeping their ability a stable secret was proving difficult, and in April he wrote to his trainer:

'I have found out from one of the letter carriers who was an accomplice in the transactions that all my correspondence both ways was regularly opened last year and that the letter carriers were in the pay of Parker, a coal merchant in Golden Square—the same parties have now got a boy in their pay whom you got from Tom Davies at Doncaster but dismissed about a month ago . . . The boy has advised his employers to back Croton Oil in the Newmarket Handicap, Strathspey for the Chester Cup and Rose of Cashmere for The Oaks.'

Meanwhile at the Newmarket Craven meeting Colonel Peel objected to an entry for the Chester Cup. The horse to which he took exception was Mr. Parry's Zanoni, one of the top weights whom, incredible though it may seem, was none other than Maccabeus, whose whereabouts after the 1844 Derby were veiled in mystery. Confirmation that Zanoni and Maccabeus were the same horse can be proved by reference to the Racing Calendars for the years 1843 and 1845. Mr. Parry, who lived at Reading, was the veterinary surgeon who investigated the age of Bloodstone after the New Stakes at Ascot the previous year, and had not owned any racehorses prior to 1845, when Sally Brown, Adonis and Zanoni ran in his name. Where he acquired Zanoni is unknown. Equally coincidental is that Sally Brown was out of the same mare as Zanoni and Lord George Bentinck's Croton Oil.

The Stewards heard the case brought by Colonel Peel, in reality acting on Lord George's behalf, but merely stated that, as they were not satisfied that the identity of Zanoni had been proved beyond all doubt, the horse should not be allowed to start for the Chester Cup, and gave it as their opinion that all bets made ante-post about him for that race should be null and void. Zanoni was, however, allowed to run in Mr. Parry's colours both at Royal Ascot in June, when he was unplaced and in the County Cup at York. It was bewildering that the horse which won the 1844 Derby, even though he was a year older than the other competitors with the exception of Leander, should have shown such deterioration, without causing more than passing comment and concern.

The members of the Jockey Club, however, were more concerned over the catering arrangements at the Rooms in Newmarket, and it was decided that, in future, dinner, including wine, dessert, malt liquor and tea would cost 20/–. Those who did not notify their intention to dine before midday were to be charged another 10/–. Those who put their name down to dine and did not do so would forfeit 10/–. Breakfast in the Coffee Rooms was 2/6 and soda and seltzer water sixpence a bottle.

Meanwhile the Goodwood-trained horses were still triumphant. The Duke of Richmond's filly Pic-Nic won the 1,000 Guineas from Lord George Bentinck's Pug, and at Epsom the Duke's filly Refraction won The Oaks, starting at 25–1, with Lord George's Miss Elis, one of the favourites, unplaced. Although disappointed by Miss Elis's failure, it had been a profitable meeting for Lord George, as Cherokee had won the Woodcote Stakes on the first day of the meeting, and on the Thursday both Croton Oil and Moonshine had won for him.

The 1845 Derby was dramatic, although by no stretch of imagination could it be compared with Running Rein's year. The favourite was Idas, the winner of the 2,000 Guineas, owned by the Earl of Stradbroke, who in the autumn of 1844 had retired from the office of Senior Steward. Second favourite was Weatherbit, owned by John Gully, the sixty-one-year-old ex-champion prize-fighter, life-long rival of William Crockford. Gully was also represented by Old England who, like Weatherbit, was trained at Danebury. Which of the two horses the Days thought the better was a matter only known to themselves—the facts being that Weatherbit had never seen a racecourse and Old England, who had been awarded the New Stakes the previous year on the disqualification of Bloodstone and had in addition won three races at Newmarket, was having his first race of the season. It was expected that the experienced Old England would be the more fancied, but the heavily-backed Weatherbit started at shorter odds.

On the Saturday prior to the Derby, John Gully learnt at Tattersalls that a commission agent from Manchester named Hargreaves, who was reputed to have nobbled Ratan, was taking all the money he could from those who wished to back Old England. Suspecting that the Days were perpetrating a fraud, Gully descended on Danebury in a fury, and by sheer force of personality so browbeat them that eventually William Day admitted that he had intended to 'make Old England safe', and that his confederates were a man named Bloodsworth and William Stebbings, whose brother had bought the real Running Rein for Levi Goodman. On Monday 26th May Gully, adopting the character of Lord George Bentinck, returned to Tattersalls and not only outlined the intended conduct of William Day, but also accused Hargreaves of being a party to the conspiracy. Whatever Hargreaves' failings, he was clever enough to realize that his only hope was to brazen the matter out, insist that he thought Old England had no chance, and challenge Gully to back his colt with him. Gully immediately accepted £2,500–£100. It was never disclosed exactly how the villains intended to nobble Old England, but at the Stewards' Inquiry it was stated that at one time it had been proposed that Stebbings should bruise the frog of Old England's foot, or else tie a silk handkerchief around the horse's leg and beat it with a stick until a sinew was sprung. The Stewards did not take long to come to their conclusions on the evidence given to them, and William Day, Stebbings and Bloodsworth were warned off Newmarket Heath. In the Derby Old England finished third to The Merry Monarch trained by the elderly John Forth. Another fancied runner was Charles Greville's colt Alarm. Alarm had made a winning début as a two year old when he won the Champagne Stakes at the Bibury Club's Stockbridge meeting the previous June. His jockey was S. Mann who less than a month earlier had ridden Running Rein in the Derby. At the start of the 1845 Derby, Alarm lashed out at The Libel who reared up and kicked Nat Flatman, Alarm's jockey, who was thrown to the ground by his frenzied mount. The riderless horse careered madly towards the Stewards' Stand and injured himself by colliding with the rails at the side of the course, thus ruining any chance he might have had in the race. Whilst this was happening Bentinck was watching the incident through his spy-glass and not enhancing his own reputation by the malicious manner in which he announced the tribulations of his cousin's horse.

There was no doubt in the minds of those who witnessed Lord George's behaviour that his dislike of Charles Greville was still intense, and equally that Greville was not prepared to accept this animosity without retaliation. The retaliation took a most unusual form and was brought about as a result of the Stewards' decision to 'warn off' William Day for his part in the attempted nobbling of Old England. The Day family were convinced that the instigator of William Day's disgrace was Bentinck, with whom the entire family were at logger-heads. They were even more convinced that he was their enemy when, shortly after the Derby, he had indirectly attempted to discredit John Day junior by referring to an incident which had occurred five years previously. At Lord George's suggestion Mr. Etwall, who was Member of Parliament for Andover, and whose colt by Mulatto out of Melody had started second favourite for the 1840 Derby and finished third, ridden by John Day junior, called upon Lord Stradbroke and informed him that Day had been offered a bribe by Mr. Crommelin to ensure the defeat of his Derby mount. It seems astonishing that this information should have been withheld for five years, and suddenly produced for no apparent reason. The 1840 Derby result could not be altered, nor could any wagers made upon it. If Lord George had known about it at the time it happened, he is unlikely to have delayed proceedings for so long. A possible reason is that Mr. Etwall mentioned the incident to Lord George when the racing world were discussing William Day's betrayal of Old England, and he seized upon it as another means of discrediting the Day family. At this moment Charles Greville believed he saw his opportunity, through Mr. Crommelin, of taking his revenge upon his cousin; for it came to his attention that, throughout the years when Bentinck's horses had been at Danebury, Lord George had written constantly to the Days, and they had kept all his letters. In his diary Greville wrote:

'In the hour of his (Crommelin's) danger the Days came in a very extraordinary manner, but very effectively to his assistance. They told him that they could furnish him with weapons which in

134

case of necessity he could wield against Lord George with terrible effect, and that if the latter persisted in pursuing him to his ruin, he might overwhelm his accuser in a destruction not less complete. They had preserved all his correspondence during the whole period of their connection, and the whole of it they now abandoned to Crommelin. He selected from the vast mass a number of important letters which he brought to me. They were damning in their import, for they disclosed a systematic course of treachery, falsehood and fraud which would have been far more than sufficient to destroy any reputation, but which would have fallen with tenfold force upon the great Purist, the supposed type and model of integrity and honour. . . . Besides this unparalleled tissue of fraud, falsehood and selfishness, the secret correspondence divulged many other things, plans and schemes of all sorts, horses who were to be made favourites in order to be betted against, not intended to win, then horses who were to run repeatedly in specified races and get beaten, till they were well handicapped in some great race which they were to run and win. . . . All these things were concocted with infinite care and explained in elaborate detail, the whole forming such a mass of roguery that any attempt at explanation, extenuation or palliation would have been in vain.'

For what reason it has never been disclosed, these letters given to Mr. Crommelin by the Days were never published, and it is a possibility that Bentinck persuaded Crommelin to destroy them. When the Stewards heard the case regarding the 1840 Derby no steps were taken to warn off Crommelin, although John Day junior was warned off.

The day before the hearing it was announced that at a meeting of noblemen and gentlemen interested in the Wood v Peel trial held at Mr. Weatherby's office, it was agreed that an appeal should be made to all those who benefited by the defeat of the Running Rein fraud, either in the shape of winnings on Orlando or by being saved from loss through the establishment of Running Rein's pretensions, to contribute a percentage upon their bets, sweepstakes or lotteries towards the legal costs of the case estimated at £3,065. It was also announced that the committee set up to manage the Bentinck Testimonial subscribed to thank

Lord George for his indefatigable exertions to expose the abuses and reform the usages of the Turf had decided, with Bentinck's consent, to use the money, amounting to £2,000, for the support and education of the children of deserving trainers and jockeys.

The Jockey Club honoured Lord George at Newmarket in July when they elected him to be one of the Stewards for the ensuing three years, in place of the Earl of Stradbroke. His fellow Stewards were the Marquis of Exeter and Col. Anson. All three must have had high hopes of winning the 1846 Derby, for Col. Anson had nominated six horses, Exeter seven and Lord George eighteen! On the same afternoon at Liverpool the Bentinck Testimonial was run, a handicap stakes with a piece of plate valued at 100 sovereigns added. On the silver salver was inscribed:

'Honourably to commemorate the public spirited exertions of Lord George Bentinck by whose zeal and perseverance a fatal blow was struck at the late irregularities and growing mal-practices of the Turf; a wholesome unflinching lesson was read to the Owners, Trainers and Riders of Horses; punctuality, order, obedience and fair play were re-established at the Starting Post, and thus to the frequenters of the Race Course, whether attracted to the National Sport by pleasure or speculation, confidence and satisfaction were secured: this Piece of Plate was given to be run over Liverpool Race-Course. July 18. 1845.'

All this inscribed on one piece of plate!

At the Goodwood meeting in July, it seemed that Lord George's star was at its zenith for, newly elected as a Steward of the Jockey Club, he was respected by the majority of race-goers as the greatest reformer the Turf had ever known. He had radically improved the standard of starts, he had done everything in his power to rid the betting fraternity of those who either would not or could not pay when they lost, and had made it exceedingly difficult for any horse to masquerade under a false name or breeding. At Goodwood, with the permission of the Duke of Richmond, he had carried out schemes which had made the racecourse the most modern in the country. He had levelled and widened the final furlong of the track by cutting into the side of the hill and broadening the narrow plateau which fell away so sharply to Charlton. Dissatisfied with the lack of control over spectators, who wandered at will, he constructed enclosures, and charged an admission fee. Under his guidance races started promptly at the scheduled time, and the names of jockeys and their racing silks appeared on racecards.

Discord won the opening race of the Goodwood meeting. In the course of the afternoon nine other horses carried Lord George's racing silks, but only one of them managed to win. The hot summer's afternoon was, however, full of incident, for after Merry Monarch, the Derby winner, was beaten a head in a 1½-mile race by a three-year-old filly giving him weight, Squire Osbaldeston rode the odds-on Sorella, his previous year's 1,000 Guineas winner, and also got beaten!

On the Wednesday Lord George Bentinck's filly Miss Elis, beaten in The Oaks, redeemed her reputation by winning the Goodwood Stakes by six lengths. Lord George determined to run her again the next day in the Goodwood Cup, ostensibly to take on John Gully's Weatherbit. Weatherbit had won at Royal Ascot and was considered unbeatable by his stable connections.

The betting on the race was as heavy as had ever been known at Goodwood, with Lord George playing up his considerable winnings on Miss Elis, who had won the Goodwood Stakes at the generous odds of 100–7, and the Danebury supporters backing Weatherbit as though he was already first past the post. Both Miss Elis and Weatherbit had a pace-maker, and in the early stages of the race Discord, in Lord George's second colours of 'blue, scarlet velvet cap' could be seen leading the field of 12 by several lengths. At the top of the hill Miss Elis was sent on past her stable companion and, coming to the final three furlongs was four lengths clear of her nearest rival. With the exception of Weatherbit her opponents were now routed, but Gully's horse was running on strongly and, making his challenge a furlong from the winning-post, got to within a length of Miss Elis—but no nearer! Bentinck's filly was still full of running and strode away to win by two lengths. So pleased was Lord George over this victory that he commissioned the famous Royal Academician Abraham Cooper to paint Miss Elis, with her jockey and trainer. He also paid for a dinner for all the Goodwood estate workers to commemorate Miss Elis's triumphs, but it was not held until after the harvest was in. Much to his trainer Kent's annoyance, Bentinck greedily decided to run Miss Elis in the Chesterfield Cup less than 24 hours after her Goodwood Cup victory. She started favourite but, tired after her previous exertions, was a beaten filly a long way from home.

The rest of the racing year was uneventful from Lord George's viewpoint, although due to his initiative Mr. Dorling announced that, in future, the Grandstand at Epsom was to be enclosed and the lawn in front of it to be sloped, railed and enlarged for the benefit of spectators. A spacious hall would be provided for use as a betting room in wet and cold weather, and two new rooms built for the use of the Jockey Club and the Bench of Local Magistrates. Another innovation proposed by Bentinck was that the horses should be saddled in front of the grandstand, and so certain was Dorling of the future profit of these improvements that he added a further £300 to the stake money for 1846.

By the end of the season Bentinck had won 58 races worth £17,372 with 25 horses. At first sight this total may seem profitable, but unless he gambled successfully on an extensive scale he had no chance of recouping his huge outlay, for his training fees amounted to £10,000, his entry fees and forfeits another £10,000 and the maintenance of his stud a further £10,000.

In September, although his filly Princess Alice won the Champagne Stakes, which cost him £75 for champagne drunk at the Turf Tavern at Doncaster by his trainer and others at a traditional celebration dinner that evening, he lost heavily, owing to his belief that Miss Sarah, who had beaten Miss Elis at York, was a 'good thing' for the St. Leger. Unfortunately she was beaten by The Baron, an Irish horse who had not been seen on an English racecourse until he ran unplaced in the Liverpool St. Leger in July. Immediately after the Doncaster race the trainer of Miss Sarah put in an objection to the winner on the grounds that he was a four year old. Examined by three veterinary surgeons the following day, The Baron was certified by them to be a three year old. Lord George won back most of his losses when his filly My Mary won the Great Yorkshire Handicap, and even more when Miss Sarah won the Park Hill Stakes on the last day of the meeting. At Welbeck during the weekend he came to the conclusion that The Baron was handicapped to win the Cesarewitch and backed him heavily. As the day of the race approached, and it seemed unlikely that any of his own horses had any chance of winning, he offered to release Nat Flatman to ride The Baron. The offer was accepted and The Baron won by a length. The following day the Newmarket starter, Mr. Perren, was 'sacked' and the Stewards of the Jockey Club appointed Mr. Hibburd of Ascot in his stead at a salary of £50 a year. Meanwhile The Baron was installed favourite for the Cambridgeshire at odds of 2–1. On the Monday before the race, a Mr. E. R. Clarke entered the Subscription Rooms at Tattersalls and informed the assembled and shocked company that he had bought The Baron and that unless he was offered the odds £12,000–£1,000 he would scratch his horse forthwith. The Baron was trained for Mr. Clarke by the infamous Henry Stebbings. To add to the general confusion Charles Greville intimated that he was undecided as to whether or not to run Alarm since he had been forestalled in the market by others. Eventually Alarm ran in the Cambridgeshire and won by two lengths ridden by Flatman, who thus brought off the autumn double.

1845 was the most profitable year that Bentinck ever enjoyed for, in addition to his gambles on The Baron, Miss Elis and My Mary, he had won a great deal of money when the Duke of Richmond's Lothario won the Liverpool Cup, and Red Deer won at Newmarket. However the more frequently his horses won, the more problems he had to face with regard to his stable security, for there were many blacklegs who would gladly pay for information about the horses trained at Goodwood. In January 1846 he wrote to Kent:

'You deserve I give you the greatest credit for the great zeal and skill and ability with which you have detected the Traitor in our stable. Now we have found him out we are fools indeed if we can't ruin him and all his gang. Of course we must continue to sham the utmost confidence in him—and then we must take good care we put him wrong in everything of any importance. It is too late to put him on the wrong scent as regards Best Bower in the Chester Cup unless we can manage it by making Miss Elis win the trials a long way. It will be too late also to attempt setting him wrong as to Blackbird and the Voluptuary colt—but I think with Nereus and Rose of Cashmere we might have a fine game.

Bell and Edmonds must both have a ride or two on Nereus half-trained so that they should be beat to the devil in all his trials. It will not be too late to deceive him about Planet: However I must leave this to you. I see you are now quite master of the game.'

This was followed up a few days later by:

'Nothing can be more clever, able or skilful than the manner in which you have discovered the misdoings of Edmonds—but it is absolutely necessary we should keep him on without allowing him to suspect that we have found him out & we will make him the most efficient tool that could be for our own purposes—I will undertake to say I will make thousands by putting him and his infernal allies on the wrong scent.—Edmonds must not on any account be discharged but the boy who tells you must be well rewarded. Edmonds must be kept right in all matter of small concernment but when we mean to do great things such as with Nereus & Rose of Cashmere & Planet in all their cases he & Bell must both be put quite in the hole, I shall have no scruples in dismissing Edmonds at any moment when I find it will best answer my purpose to do so.

. . . The way Colonel Anson & John Scott saved first Attila & then Cotherstone from being poisoned was by sending the head lad in the one case & the boy in the other, who were to do the job, suddenly away to fetch a horse from Malton so that there was no suspicion that he had discovered the conspiracy was excited—& the consequence in both cases was that the whole gang of conspirators was entirely ruined.

In like manner we must make excuses for getting Edmonds out of the way when occasion requires it.—Sometimes we can do so by ordering him to ride some weight we know he cannot ride, and then taking him off at the last moment.'

It was difficult for the touts to beat Lord George, but on one occasion at Goodwood they managed to spoil his plans. At dawn the week before the July meeting, Bentinck went on to the gallops to watch one of his three-year-old fillies put through her paces. She was a 50–1 chance for a stakes race, but Kent had assured her owner that she ought to win, and provided she proved her ability that morning Bentinck confidently expected to win a small fortune, so great were the odds. Before the trial started Bentinck saw an elderly woman collecting mushrooms at the side of the gallop and kindly rode up to warn her not to get in the way of the horses. The woman looked up, put her hand to her ear affecting deafness and held up the basket of mushrooms, which Lord George took, throwing her five shillings in exchange.

The trial was brilliantly successful, with the filly winning in a canter and Lord George rode back to Goodwood House in a very happy frame of mind. He immediately sent letters to London ordering his commissioners to back the filly, and decided later in the morning to ride to the Swan Hotel at Chichester, where he was staying, to stake some more wagers with the local betting men. To his astonishment he arrived in Chichester to learn that his filly was such a favourite for the race that no one wished to lay her at any price.

All day the stable lads, the jockeys and even Kent himself were questioned by Bentinck in his efforts to discover how the secret of the trial had leaked out, but to no avail. The following morning he was horrified to hear from London that his commission agents had also been forestalled and instead of booking the expected £10,000–£200, they had only managed to take £1,600–£200, proving conclusively that news of the trial had reached London very quickly. Bentinck, still mystified, was given the solution at breakfast when the waiter said 'I have had the mushrooms stewed, my Lord, which your Lordship's groom gave me yesterday. They are very fine indeed, my Lord'. The duped Bentinck rose to feet, sending breakfast crockery flying, as he exclaimed 'And so they ought to be! That horrid old woman was the culprit, and this hateful dish has cost me £8,400, independent of the five shillings I gave the old harridan, or strictly speaking, some tout in disguise.'

To rub salt into the wound, the filly won at Goodwood the following week, leading from start to finish.

In the early summer months of 1846 the Repeal of the Corn

Laws occupied the attention of the nation. Mr. Gully's filly Mendicant won the 1,000 Guineas and The Oaks and his colt, Pyrrhus the First, won the Derby, to give him a memorable Epsom double. Charles Greville's Alarm won the Ascot Gold Cup.

The Goodwood races in July were established as one of the highlights of the sporting and social year and, as was customary, a few of the Duke and Duchess of Richmond's closest friends, including Lord George Bentinck, arrived on the Saturday previous to the meeting. During the week-end more than one hundred racehorses were brought to the vicinity by their trainers, and even those who were not stabled at Goodwood were allowed to use the gallops for their final work-outs. By Monday evening all the Goodwood house-party had arrived and at dinner the table was decorated with gold and silver racing-cups won by the Duke's horses. When the ladies retired the men brought out their betting books and the following day's card was called over amongst them. Traditionally, the proposing of the Duke's health, by the highest ranking guest present at the dinner, was held over until Cup day.

Every day throughout the week, as the stable clock struck twelve o'clock, the Duke's carriages arrived at the front door to take the guests to the races. There was a close carriage and four, the postillions in red and white striped jackets, the footmen in white and red liveries, turned up with silver and turned down with yellow. Behind the carriage came an open landau, a brougham, a phaeton, and for those energetic enough horses on which they could canter up the hill through the park to the grandstand, where lunch, sent up from Goodwood House, was served to the Duke's guests.

On the first day George Payne and Bentinck rode up together, discussing the rumour that one of the favourites for the Cup was to be nobbled that night. They agreed that it was not a case for the local police, and decided to call upon the services of one of His Majesty's Theatre commissionaires who, because of his knowledge of the London pick-pockets and mobsmen, was considered a suitable nightwatchman for the horse.

The sensation of the racing year came after dinner at Goodwood House on the third day of the meeting, when the Duke had led his male guests into the small library. In this room with its elegant gallery, balustraded in bronze, and with historic furniture which included a writing-desk chair of Napoleon, Bentinck seemed strangely silent as the house-party discussed the chances of their horses on the morrow. His friends knew that he had suffered an arduous summer in the House of Commons, and seemed exhausted. They knew too that he seldom appeared elated by the victories of his horses, and did not expect him to crow over the fact that, of the 30 horses he had already run at the meeting, Planet and Slander had finished first and second in the Molecomb Stakes, that Best Bower had won the Goodwood Stakes and that Dawdle, Coal Black Rose and Devil Me Care had also won, any more than they expected him to be disconsolate at the defeat of Crozier, who had been trounced by a horse trained at Danebury. As the evening wore on, and Lord Chesterfield, flushed with wine, drank toast after toast to his horse Lady Wildair, who had won the Stewards Cup with Lord George's filly Dawdle second, Lord George maintained his silence. He drank far less than most of the others and smoked not at all.

Quite suddenly he rose from his chair and to everyone's astonishment said 'Will anyone give me £10,000 for all my lot, beginning with Bay Middleton and ending with little Kitchener, and take over their engagements?' Lord George was not the man to ask such a question in frivolity. He was not drunk, nor was he joking, but the thought that the largest stable in the country should be virtually given away, for no apparent reason, was beyond the comprehension of his fellow guests. The sum mentioned of £10,000 was a trifle to many of them, no more than the winnings of a day at the races or a night at the card table. Yet they were overawed by the magnitude of the proposition. George Payne was the first to regain his composure, and requested that if he could have an option on the horses until noon he would pay £300 forfeit if he declined Lord George's offer. From Payne's point-of-view there were two problems if he bought the Bentinck horses lock, stock and barrel. Firstly, who would train them? His own trainer, Montgomery Dill, would not have been equal to so gigantic an undertaking. Secondly, where would they be trained? This was less difficult to solve, for John Forth was leaving Michel Grove, near Arundel, and the establishment was large enough to accommodate all the horses. Bentinck advised Payne to approach John Kent, but Kent, far too loyal to desert the Duke of Richmond, refused to consider the proposal, even though Payne offered him £500 a year more than he was being paid at that time. If Kent would not train for him at Michel Grove, the project was too involved to appeal to George Payne, and the responsibilities of owning the largest racing establishment in the land too burdensome. At the races the following afternoon gossip had it that Mr. Payne had bought the Bentinck horses, and his decision to do so was made to look even wiser by the victories of three of Lord George's horses, including his filly, Princess Alice, who won the Nassau Stakes. For once gossip was wrong, as Payne had given Lord George his cheque for £300 before they had left Goodwood House. Inevitably, when the news leaked out that the sale to Payne had fallen through, the speculation as to what would happen became the sole topic of conversation. It was rumoured that Henry Padwick, the moneylender and bookmaker, would willingly pay the asked for £10,000, but the least knowledgeable of race-goers knew that Lord George would never sell to such a man for any price.

Amongst the Duke of Richmond's house-guests was the Hon. Edward Mostyn, who had inherited the dam of Queen of Trumps, the 1835 St. Leger winner, from his bachelor uncle, Sir Thomas Mostyn, described by Nimrod as 'A single man, possessed of a fine fortune', who at one time had hunted the Bicester country. The Mostyns were a Flintshire family, and their racehorses were trained at Holywell on gallops which adjoined the racecourse. Edward Mostyn's father had been elected Member for Flintshire on the death of his brother-in-law in 1831, and knew Bentinck in the House of Commons. Forty-year-old Edward Mostyn shared his father's love of racing, and his friendship with the Duke of Richmond resulted in the invitation to stay at Goodwood. He already had many horses in training, but this did not deter him from proposing to Lord George that he took over all his horses on one condition, that the horses could remain at Goodwood under the care of Kent for as long as he wished.

28. Epsom scenes, 1848

THE START.—THEY'RE OFF.

They're off! they're off! the shout, the cry,
Extend along the plain;
And countless hearts are beating high,
And countless eyeballs strain!

Echo rolling and resounding loud—
Are heard afar—now near!
Yes, here they are! the gallant steeds
Swift as the wind appear.

They're passed! they're passed! the race is won
Huzza! the winner's Cotherstone!

JOCKEYS MOUNTED.

"Observed of all observers!" bright array!
In all the hues the rainbow doth display;
Silent and stern, with brow and lip compressed,
As men on whom an empire's fortunes rest;
And who have braced their minds some deed to dare
Which shall to future times their memories bear.
Distinguished is your lot and proud your mien;
In stature small, but heroes of the scene.

AFTER THE RACE.

It is after the race—
What a change on each face!
Some nigh weeping, some laughing, some swearing—
Some down-hearted go home—
To the play-booths some roam,
In the hope their ill luck of repairing;
While some play roulette
And find that they get
Into a worse state than they were in.

RETURNING HOME.

The monster-crowd is homeward bound
A thousand cries the ear confound;
The noise of whips and wheels resound—
Bustle and clamour reign around.

And friends are lost and friends are found
Amid the dense array,
All haste to town! the flats done brown!

The rich, the poor, the gay,
All are whirled on their way,
But will not soon forget

The bustle and the bet,
The varied incidents they met,
Epsom the Derby day!

29. Epsom scenes, 1848

After consultation with the Duke of Richmond the transaction was agreed upon and Mostyn found himself the owner of three stallions, 50 horses in training, 70 brood mares, 50 yearlings, and 45 foals, all for the insignificant sum of £10,000. Amongst the yearlings was a dark bay by Touchstone out of Lord George's great mare Crucifix who had been named Surplice.

The sale was the talking-point of the racing world for the whole of August, and countless reasons were put forward for Bentinck's decision to give up his racing empire. The majority of the opinions based their assumptions on pressure of his political work as the cause of the sale. The minority suggested that he felt his life's work as a Turf reformer was completed. A reason appreciated by very few was his lack of finance to continue to race on so lavish a scale, but this reason was stressed in a letter he wrote, early in September, to his brother William John who, like his other brothers and sisters, always addressed him as 'Singe':

'My stud will prove a wonderful bargain to the purchasers. I have no doubt but that they would have realized £15,000 clear if they had sold everything, but I always estimated that they would sell for £5,000 more in anybody's else's hands than mine. They have refused 7,000 gns for Planet & Slander & I was told 3,000 gns for *three bar those two*, & they have already sold 33 lots for 3,700 guineas (there were 205 lots in all). I fancy they mean to sell nothing worth keeping except at extortionate prices—They sold Comrade for 200 gns—He has been begging for 3 months at 50 gns—he is a crib-biter—a roarer—& frequently breaks a blood-vessel in the head & falls consequently without notice in his gallops!! Old "Phantasima"—now past breeding sold for 17 gns—last year when heavy in foal to Emilius no one at the hammer bid 5 gns for her.

I see Crozier was put up at 400 gns & I believe they might have got 600 or 700 guineas for him with his engagements— last year I put him up at the hammer at Tattersalls to be sold for a guinea if it was bid—it would have been happy for me if some-one had bought him for a guinea—but no one would bid half a guinea for him! ! !

I regret Planet more even than Crucifix.—Planet is a better horse than ever Crucifix has yet bred. However I should have liked to have kept them both—but I knew if I kept anything back the stud would not sell at all. I was dying to be out of it—they were costing me £40 a day & when I gave away the 200 Sovereign stake to Gully & John Day through mismanagement in running Crozier instead of Planet for it I was so disgusted & so satisfied I must be ruined if I went on with a racing establishment without having time to look after it & attend to it myself that I felt quite a load off my mind as soon as they were sold for £10,000 —though I had valued them in my own mind in consultation with Kent at 23,000 gns with their engagements.

I owed Drummond's £17,000—I have paid them off £7,000 & mean to pay them off the remaining £10,000 at Christmas when Mostyn is to pay me for the stud—unless you will let me pay off the £7,000 I owe you (exclusive of the interest I ought to have paid but never have paid you for God knows how many years).

You need have no scruple in the matter because I shall now have more income than I shall know well how to spend & will bear in mind the Duke of Richmond owes me £10,000 in bond. In short I think the money is more wanted by you & would be turned to better account by you now than by me.

ever yours most affectionately

George Bentinck.'

Although pressure of political work may have affected his decision to sell his horses, the fact remains that he had been Member of Parliament for King's Lynn for 18 years before he made any impact upon the House of Commons. Two years after his election he had withdrawn his support from the Duke of Wellington's Government when Canning left the Administration, and on the accession of Lord Grey's ministry he refused to accept a post in the Government, giving as his reason pressure of other interests! His visits to the House were infrequent and when, towards the end of Lord Melbourne's Government in 1841, the two political parties were evenly balanced and his vote was needed at divisions, he often arrived direct from Danebury, late in the evening, with his hunting clothes only partially hidden by a white great-coat. Many of the aristocratic members of the House were his personal friends, and whatever their political opinions, they shared sporting interests with him. He intended no disrespect when treating the House of Commons more as a social club than as a Senate. He supported the Reform Bill whole-heartedly, but had no desire to associate himself with the middle-class Parliamentarians which it brought in its wake. They might think him a snob, but their opinions totally disinterested him and he disregarded them. His racing activities gave him little time for literary pursuits and he seldom read a book, yet he had a prodigious memory and used to say 'I don't pretend to know much, but I do know men and horses'. His political decisions were made promptly and, although he might be accused of being prejudiced against individuals, he had no prejudice against 'things'. Once his mind was made up, no one could persuade him to change it.

His greatest personal friend in the House of Commons was Lord Stanley, to whose grandfather the 12th Earl of Derby, the Epsom Classics owe their names—the one race bearing his title, the other the name of his Epsom residence, The Oaks. The 12th Earl had married the famous actress Miss Farren, who had played in Sheridan's 'School for Scandal' and out of compliment to her had named one of his horses Sir Peter Teazle. In 1787 this horse gave the Earl the first victory in the Derby of the 'black white cap'. His grandson was born at Knowsley in March 1799, two years before the birth of Lord George. After following the almost ritual education of Eton and Christ Church, at the age of 23 he was elected as Member for Stockbridge, and thus found Danebury in his constituency. He spent considerably more time in Parliamentary debate than did Bentinck, and was a far more able orator than Lord George, who had neither a strong voice nor a fluent manner. The majority of his horses were trained by John Scott at Malton, but it was not until the latter half of the nineteenth century that his famous colours began to win Classic races although he had enjoyed the atmosphere of the racecourse ever since he left Christ Church. In 1851, only a year before he became Prime Minister, Greville described him at Newmarket:

'There he was in the midst of a crowd of blacklegs, betting men and loose characters of every description, in uproarious spirits, chaffing, rowing and shouting with laughter and joking. Here was a statesman without inhibitions, a sportsman without exclusion, a countryman with as firm a tread on the Turf as any banker in his counting-house, a churchman as completely at his ease in contemplating the racecourse as in championing the cause of Altar & Throne.'

In 1841 on the defeat of Lord Melbourne, Bentinck was once more offered an administrative Government post, and Sir Robert Peel, Colonel Jonathan Peel's elder brother, astutely asked Lord Stanley to make the offer to him personally, in the hope that his persuasive powers would overcome any lack of enthusiasm. Lord Stanley failed, as Lord George adamantly insisted that he could not spare the time, although he promised his support to Peel's Government. This he did until the momentous political days in 1845 and 1846, which culminated in the Repeal of the Corn Laws. When Sir Robert Peel proposed an Order in Council suspending restrictions placed upon corn importation, in his efforts to counteract the failure of the potato crop in Ireland and the danger of insufficient corn in England, Bentinck was appalled. Later, when Peel avowed that such an Order should remain as its repeal would be inexpedient, Bentinck considered that Peel had betrayed the country, and campaigned for the maintenance of protective duties. In private he told his friends, 'Well, I keep racehorses in three counties, and they tell me I shall save £1,500 a year by Free Trade. I don't care for that. What I cannot bear is being sold.' He worked incessantly preparing facts, figures and statistics to support the Protectionists' case, and delivered his speech at the most inauspicious moment. The House of Commons had been debating the Corn Laws for twelve days, and the subject itself and the members were exhausted. Lord George, inexperienced in oratory, rose to address the House, long after midnight. As was his custom, he had not eaten since his breakfast of dry toast, but his nervous energy gave him reserves of strength, and he impressed the House with his sincerity, as well as with the mountain of economic facts and figures he laid before them. He claimed that he was fighting the battle of a party whose leaders had deserted them, and trusted that the House would remember the emergency which had dragged him out to intrude upon their indulgence. He also objected in his speech to the fact that Sir Robert Peel had persuaded the Prince Consort to listen to the first night of this crucial debate. At the end of his speech, certainly the most important he had ever made, he said:

'If we are a proud aristocracy, we are proud of our honour, in as much as we never have been guilty and never can be guilty, of double-dealing with the farmers of England—of swindling our opponents, deceiving our friends, or betraying our constituents.'

When the House voted, at nearly four o'clock in the morning, the Protectionist amendment was defeated, but out of the 581 members who voted, 242 voted against the Bill.

Lord George's style of speaking could never be acclaimed as attractive, he was inclined to ramble and to repeat himself, his actions were over theatrical and his voice high pitched. At political meetings in his constituency of King's Lynn he was inclined 'after humming away for ½ hour in a voice almost inaudible, to gain a little more courage and occupy an hour more wearying his audience with sentences slowly dragged forth.' He loathed the speeches required from him at the opening of bazaars and agricultural shows. Another loathing of his was the social grace of dancing, and the thought of spending a few hours in an Assembly Hall politely waltzing and gavotting with his female constituents sent him into the depths of misery. Nevertheless, if his speeches were read and not listened to, they were first class in material, and appealed to the country, if not to the House of Commons. He had one particular asset, and that was that his social prestige, and the influence of his father, the Duke of Portland, always guaranteed him a hearing.

Throughout the spring of 1846, Lord George worked tirelessly for the cause of the Protectionists. He violently attacked Sir Robert Peel, and during the Easter recess accepted the leadership of the Protectionist Party, on the condition that he would relinquish his leadership as soon as a suitable successor was found.

In a letter he wrote:

'Virtually an uneducated man, never intended or attracted by taste for political life, in the House of Commons only by a pure accident, indeed by an inevitable and undesired change, I am well aware of my own incapability to fill the station I have been thrust into. My sole ambition was to rally the broken and disspirited forces of a betrayed & insulted party, and to avenge the country gentlemen & landed aristocracy of England upon the minister who, presuming on their weakness, falsely flattered himself that they could be trampled on with impunity. I own I am bitterly disappointed and broken hearted that England has proved to be so degenerate that, in face of an emergency, she has produced, as far as I can see, no new leaders to take my place.'

The reason why Lord George was reluctant to lead any political party was that, in his own opinion, he had not the necessary qualifications. As a young man he had been dazzled by the brilliance of his uncle by marriage, George Canning, and he felt that any political leader ought to have at least as many attributes as Canning possessed. Another complex reason was his personal belief in religious liberty, based upon the part that his ancestors had played in the expulsion of the Stuart monarchs. His belief ran contrary to the views of many Parliamentarians with whom he might otherwise have been in accord. In a letter to his father he explained his fears that he might have to lead the House of Commons, a task for which he thought he was quite unfitted. Whether or not the Duke of Portland thought this, one certainty is that Lord George's belief that Peel had betrayed the nation was no stronger than that held by his father who, four years later, as Peel was dying, wrote 'I am quite sure it would have been a good thing if he had never been born'.

13

The last horses ever to run in Lord George Bentinck's colours were the filly Slander and the colt Vice Consul. Strictly they were the property of Edward Mostyn, but they both ran in the Prince of Wales Stakes at York before there was time to substitute the Mostyn colours of 'yellow, black cap'. Slander won by a length from George Payne's Clementina which earned Kent the teasing rebuke from her owner 'So you have beaten me the first time you ran against me after refusing to become my trainer'.

The Monday after York races Mostyn went to Goodwood to discuss the sale of the majority of Lord George's horses. There was a suggestion that a mammoth sale should take place at Goodwood, but the idea did not meet with the Duke of Richmond's approval. Consequently on September 7th a draft of thirty lots, consisting of nineteen brood mares, three yearlings and eight horses in training were sold at Tattersalls for £3,720. In October the Stewards of the Jockey Club adjudicated a case brought by the Marquess of Exeter who had a fifth retainer on the jockey Abdale. He claimed that the fact that Mostyn had bought Lord George's horses did not entitle him to precedence for Abdale's services. There was no animosity between Lord Exeter and Mostyn who maintained that he had a prior claim. The Stewards, who included Lord George, found in favour of Lord Exeter.

The end of the year saw the sale of further batches of Lord George's horses by Mostyn who wisely refused to contemplate the sale of Surplice. Writing to his former trainer from Welbeck Abbey, on Christmas day, Lord George commented:

'If you have really got a good horse in Surplice you should

persuade the Duke to put £100 or £200 upon him now at long odds. Let the Duke once take an interest in one of Mr. Mostyn's horses as a Derby horse, he will be as anxious about him as if he were his own and as unwilling as I should be to see them leave Goodwood. I who stood to win above £100,000 at one time was scarcely more excited about Gaper than the Duke was before the Derby, having backed him to win £5,000 or £6,000. The Duke likes standing the odds to £200 for the Derby at long odds about a horse he knows something about ...... Mr. Mostyn, I believe, never bets a shilling ...'

During February 1847, the Duke of Richmond sold Red Deer, and Squire Osbaldeston sold The Saddler, who was exported to Bohemia and died at Ostend after a terrible journey across the North Sea. Nevertheless, during the winter there was plenty of money ante-post for the 1847 Derby for Mr. Mostyn's Planet who was favourite for the Epsom Classic, until his defeat by Conyngham in the 2,000 Guineas.

Two incidents at the Chester meeting in May caused comment. Crockford's son lodged a protest against William Scott being allowed to start his horse Erin-go-Bragh for the Chester Cup, as he claimed that Scott had not settled an outstanding debt of £300 owed to him over the 1846 Derby. He maintained that the Goodwood articles concerning defaulting, drawn up by Bentinck, applied to Chester, but the Stewards over-ruled his objection. More ingenious was the villainy of a gentleman who hired a special express train to take him from Chester to catch a connection to Peterborough where, by means of the Eastern Counties Electric Telegraph, he got news of the Chester Cup result to his London confederates two hours before the official news seeped through. Two hours in which to make a fortune!

On the eve of the Derby, Lord George proposed a motion in the House of Commons that 'The House at its rising do adjourn until Thursday', thus originating the Parliamentary tradition that there is a holiday on Derby Day.

The Derby was won by Cossack, owned by John Gully's son-in-law, and trained by the Days at Danebury. Mostyn had four runners in the race, including Planet and Crozier, but none of his horses distinguished themselves. Nevertheless, as the summer months sped by, his two-year-old colt Surplice pleased his trainer, and gave promise of becoming a top-class colt.

Surplice was a dark bay horse with very black legs, standing a little more than 16.1 hands, and even as a two year old was an impressive looking thoroughbred. Like so many other brilliant horses he was lazy in his home gallops, and kept his best performances for the racecourse. His début was made in the Ham Produce Stakes in even greater style. In this race, Loadstone, also owned by Mostyn and bred by Bentinck, was a runner, but did not 'trouble' the judge. His jockey, Frank Butler, thought that he could have defeated Surplice and in consequence told Colonel Anson, who had a retainer on his services, that Surplice might not be the world-beater that people believed. It proved expensive advice for Colonel Anson who, after dinner that evening at Goodwood House, offered £15,000–£2,000 against Surplice for the following year's Derby. The bet was accepted by Lord Enfield, the Duke of Richmond's brother-in-law, and Colonel Anson then halved his liability by allowing the Hon. Francis Villiers, 28-year-old son of the Earl of Jersey, to share the bet with him. Villiers had only recently returned from abroad where he had served with his regiment for ten years. He was extravagant, profligate, reckless and with few scruples, and even worse had a burning ambition to make a fortune at the expense of the bookmakers.

At Doncaster Surplice enhanced his reputation by winning the Municipal Stakes at 10–1 on, a price which appealed to Admiral Rous who only liked betting on 'certainties' and wagered £100. In the first October meeting at Newmarket Surplice 'walked over' and was installed winter favourite for the Derby at a price of 11–1 which had shortened to 9–1 by March 1848. The winter was excessively cold and not to the liking of many trainers who found difficulty in preparing their horses for the Spring meetings. Pleasure was found in the cold weather, however, by two teams of cricket enthusiasts who played an unusual game of cricket on skates at Chatsworth, home of the Duke of Devonshire.

During the winter months in the House of Commons Lord George was busily engaged as Chairman of the Parliamentary committee set up to consider the interests of the sugar and coffee planters. He advocated protective duties on foreign sugar, but his resolution was rejected. In July 1847 he had written to Croker discussing the chances of success in the House of Commons:

. . .'But I am a jockey, and it is the first principle of our craft to be satisfied with winning the race, if it is only by a head, and never to risk losing by showing off how much farther it might have been won.'

On Boxing Day he commented on the fact:

'I have ceased to be leader of the House of Commons Opposition. My vote & speech on the New Bill gave dire offence to the party, and on Monday I got a long letter . . . the long and short of which was an intimation that for daring to make that speech I must be prepared to receive my dismissal. . . . Appointed on account of my uncompromising Spirit, I am dismissed for the same reason, that which was my principal virtue in 1846 is my damning vice in 1847.'

Significantly, he also wrote to a fellow Member of Parliament at the end of the year:

'Confidentially, I tell you, that far from feeling the least annoyed, I shall feel greatly relieved by a restoration to privacy & freedom. I worked upon my spirit in 1846 & 1847, but I have learnt now that I have shaken my constitution to the foundations, & I seriously doubt my being able to work on much longer. . . .'

If he had had time to appreciate the nefarious activities at Goodwood he would have been both angry and disgusted. Young Francis Villiers and Colonel Anson had bought Blaze, considered one of John Scott's best two year olds, in the autumn of 1847 and had backed him heavily for the 2,000 Guineas. Villiers had wagered equally heavily on Mostyn's Loadstone for the Derby. In March 1848 he persuaded Mostyn to sell a share in Loadstone and Surplice to his friend Lord Clifden. The Mostyn fortunes were at a low ebb and, from their point-of-view, the sale was very necessary. No sooner was the sale completed than, to John Kent's consternation he was informed that Loadstone and Surplice were to be scratched from the 2,000 Guineas, to ensure Blaze's victory. Villiers misguidedly had also made up his mind, based on the opinions of others, that Loadstone was a better Derby proposition than Surplice. News of Villiers' support of Loadstone reached Lord George, who wrote to Kent asking him if he still believed

Surplice to be the superior horse, in view of Villiers' wagers. The harassed trainer, thoroughly upset and disliking intensely the youthful arrogance of Villiers, was to an extent mollified when Blaze was trounced in the 2,000 Guineas, for which there were only five runners. Lord George was present at the Newmarket Guineas meeting where Colonel Anson's wife was overheard telling him that if he did not give up the stress and strain of his political activities, they would be the death of him. Whilst the Newmarket meeting was held, news was received of the deaths of two of those who had played their part in the 1844 Derby, for John Forth and Tom Ferguson had died a few weeks earlier.

Meanwhile Surplice continued to please Kent, although rumours were heard at Goodwood that Mr. John Bowes' Springy Jack would take an immensity of beating at Epsom. At Tattersalls he was so heavily backed that, by the beginning of May, he was joint favourite for the Derby with Surplice.

A fortnight before the Derby Villiers persuaded Kent to hold a trial at Goodwood over a distance of 1½ miles. Surplice was to give Loadstone 2 pounds. Also in the trial were Lord Chesterfield's Lady Wildair, Sylvan, a stable companion of the 2,000 Guineas winner Flatcatcher, and Sagacity, a useful four year old. It was Villiers' hope that Loadstone would win in impressive style, and thus make his enormous wagers on the Derby look a shrewd and wise investment. To his dismay Surplice won in a canter, with Loadstone last! It spelt financial ruin for Villiers since, if the trial was genuine, Surplice was virtually a certainty for the Derby. Once the news of the trial leaked out, the price of Surplice would so shorten that he would have to have some £25,000 on the favourite to cover his liabilities, including the £15,000–£2,000 that he and Colonel Anson had laid Lord Enfield in the autumn of 1847.

Information concerning Surplice's brilliant trial was learned by the bookmakers on the eve of Bath races, and no matter how short the odds they offered, they were accepted by Villiers' commission agent. Others who stood to lose should Surplice win the Derby followed in his wake, until Surplice became an even-money chance.

At Goodwood every precaution was taken to prevent any doper

or nobbler 'getting at' either Surplice or Loadstone, and both horses were removed from their boxes in the main stable block adjoining Goodwood House and taken to the kennels where many of Kent's hacks were kept. Here the Derby favourite and his stable companion were given every feed of corn and every bucket of water by the hand of their trainer personally. On Monday 23rd May, two days before the Derby, Surplice and Loadstone were boxed for Epsom under the supervision of Kent and the Chichester police. The Derby favourite spent the final hours before the race in the stables which Lord George had retained at Headley after he sold his horses to Mostyn.

Eleventh hour drama was caused by George Payne insisting that Nat Flatman, whom he retained, rode Glendower in his 'black and white striped' colours, for it left Surplice without a jockey. There was a suggestion that Robinson should have the mount, but the Duke of Rutland claimed him for The Fiddler. Finally Sim Templeman, who had won the 1847 Derby on Cossack, was engaged. The unusual fact about Surplice was that he was a very unpopular favourite in the hours before the Derby, entirely due to the manner in which Francis Villiers had backed Loadstone and layed against Surplice throughout the winter. Many people thought that they had been cheated.

At long last when it was appreciated that, bar an accident, Surplice was an assured Derby winner, a great number of people realized that they would suffer severe financial loss by his victory. There was every incentive for certain black-legs to prevent him starting in the race, and in consequence the security precautions, both at Goodwood and at Epsom, were on an unprecedented scale. Bentinck had backed Surplice at long odds before Christmas, and was one of those who stood to gain if he was triumphant.

The 1848 Derby was the first run over the new course, which had been devised by the Epsom licensee, Mr. Dorling, at the suggestion of Lord George, who was one of the Stewards of the Meeting. The difference was that the start of the race was now in Langley Bottom, in sight of the thousands in the Grandstands, and the uphill ascent to the top of Tattenham Corner steeper than in previous years.

There were seventeen runners for the Derby and, as they paraded in front of the stands, no one watched Surplice with more mixed feelings than Lord George Bentinck. Five years earlier, when Gaper had run in his colours, he stood to win so much money that the bookmakers would have been sore pressed to settle. Since then many of the villainous personalities of the Turf had been cast aside, and outwardly the racing of Victorian England seemed less corrupt than at any other time in history. Yet, from Lord George's viewpoint, much of the exhilaration had gone from the Turf. The excitement of the witch-hunt of a wrong-doer and the plans and schemes to bring off a gambling *coup* by defeating the handicapper and the bookmaker, had lost their attraction. Perhaps it was because he had had a surfeit of such a life, perhaps it was because of his immersion, heart and soul, in his political activities, perhaps it was that he was forty-six years of age and was exhausted. Whatever the reason the sight of Surplice, bred by him from his wonderful mare Crucifix, filled him with less emotion as he watched the Derby favourite parade in front of the stands then when he had felt his heart beating with excitement as Gaper strode down to the post in 1843.

Surplice had looked magnificent before the race, and seemed to outclass the two second favourites, George Payne's Glendower and J. B. Day's Nil Desperandum. Springy Jack, in the colours of John Bowes, caused much favourable comment and so did Loadstone, but few looked further than Surplice for the winner.

For once, the runners were off to a perfect start, with The Fowler leading the field, followed by Loadstone who took up the running after three furlongs, setting a slow pace. Surplice was moving easily, well placed just behind the front rank, and once the straight was reached was sent into the lead. Disaster nearly overtook the favourite at this moment, for he began to run lazily, and despite all Templeman's efforts he started to sprawl and lose his action. Springy Jack was brought up to challenge him inside the final furlong, but the challenge inspired Surplice to run on, and he held on gamely to win by a neck.

Amidst all the fervour of celebrations after the race as the Goodwood contingent, headed by the Duke of Richmond together with Lord Clifden and Edward Mostyn, received the congratulations of their friends, there were many who appreciated the mood of Lord George Bentinck. They knew that two days before the Derby his efforts in the House of Commons to persuade the Government to enforce protective duties on foreign sugar had been rejected, after months of ceaseless toil on his part. It was understandable therefore, that, on the day after the Derby as he stood dejectedly in the library of the House of Commons, Disraeli should have tried to console him in his double disappointment of failing in his efforts to defeat the Government and not owning the Derby winner. In his misery Lord George retorted that Disraeli did not know the importance of the Derby, to which the future Prime Minister made the now-famous reply 'It is the blue riband of the Turf'. Within a month Lord George, who had been energetically attacking the Government front bench, was rebuked by Lord John Russell who said 'These mean frauds, these extremely dishonourable tricks which the noble Lord imputes to them, are not the faults and characteristics of men high in public office in the country. They are the characteristics of men who are engaged in pursuits which the noble Lord has long followed.'

'Has long followed'; the Prime Minister's words must have conjured up many memories in Lord George's mind. It was twenty-four years since he had first ridden at Goodwood and eleven since the birth of his beloved filly Crucifix. Goodwood was now established as one of the foremost racecourses in England, and the Turf was rid of the majority of the scoundrels who had brought it into such ill-repute. His term of office as a Steward of the Jockey Club was over, and at the annual meeting held at Newmarket in July his great friend, Lord Stanley, was appointed in his place. Francis Villiers was present at the meeting, but Bentinck ignored him. One of Lord George's final acts as a Steward was to agree that judges should only receive presents from the winning owners of five races—£50 for the Derby, £30 for The Oaks, Cambridgeshire and Cesarewitch and £10 for the 2,000 Guineas.

Surplice's Derby victory was not the only triumph to rekindle his interest in the Turf, as his interest in politics waned. Chesterfield, an own brother to Crucifix, had raced once, being beaten in a humble race at Aberystwyth, before being sent to stud and had only a few poor-quality mares sent to him. One of them, Grace Darling, produced a chesnut foal of whom so little was thought that, at Bath races in 1843, the two horses, mother and son, were sold for 15 sovereigns. The son, named The Hero, proved the 'glorious uncertainty' of racing, for this apparently valueless racehorse won eleven races in 1846, ten in 1847 including the Gold Vase and the Gold Cup at Ascot, and the Cup at Goodwood, and in 1848 repeated his Ascot Gold Cup triumph. Lord George was intrigued also by details of a case heard at Maidstone, for the endless squabbles amongst the black-legs over their bets on Running Rein and Orlando were still not completed, and Stebbings was suing the infamous Ignatius Coyle for £700. Perjury was the order of the day, but after the jury found in favour of Stebbings, Coyle pleaded that he was insolvent!

Surplice was beaten twice at Goodwood in July, and in August was removed from Kent's care, together with all the other horses owned by Mostyn and Lord Clifden and sent to Robert Stephenson at Newmarket. Surplice had many adherents for the St. Leger, despite his listless displays at Goodwood, and despite support for the Duke of Bedford's Justice of Ireland and Lord Stanley's Canezou, winner of the 1,000 Guineas and the Ebor St. Leger.

Lord George had travelled up to Welbeck Abbey the week before the St. Leger meeting and spent much of his time discussing the disease of the potato crop with his father's head gardener. For days the weather had been very hot, and the Doncaster racecourse as dry as a bone. On the eve of the meeting the heavens opened, the rains came and the arid dust on the track, kicked up by the horses in their training gallops, was softened to perfect going. The Saturday before the meeting several of the St. Leger horses, including Surplice and Justice to Ireland, were taken to Euston station and put on the train for Doncaster. Towards the end of the journey there was nearly a disaster, for the front axle of one of the trucks snapped, and the horse-box, containing Justice to Ireland, which had been loaded onto the truck, toppled over.

On the first day of the Doncaster meeting Lord George was pleased at the performance of Lord Eglington's two-year-old The Flying Dutchman, sired by Bay Middleton, who won the

Champagne Stakes in a canter. St. Leger day opened dramatically for the news spread through the town like wildfire that Robinson, although engaged to ride Surplice, had refused the mount. His reputation as a jockey was high, his integrity was second to none and it was rumoured that he was unhappy at the thought of riding for Lord Clifden and Francis Villiers after his defeats on Surplice at Goodwood, and thought that it would be advisable for him to relinquish the mount in the St. Leger, so that in any event his reputation would not be in jeopardy. Nat Flatman was engaged to ride in his stead.

To the delight of Lord George a two year old by Bay Middleton won the first race, and a horse owned by George Payne was successful in the second. The third race was won by a two year old, also sired by Bay Middleton, owned by Lord Clifden, from horses owned by Bentinck's companions, Lord Glasgow, George Payne, Lord Chesterfield and Colonel Anson. Together they watched the St. Leger parade before the nine runners stood quietly at the starting gate whilst Mr. Hibburd ordered them to come up into line. There was only one false start—for which the jockeys were fined £5 subsequently reduced to £3 and a warning—before they were 'off'. At the mile-post Flatcatcher, the 2,000 Guineas winner was setting a furious pace, followed at a distance of four lengths by Surplice and Canezou. Inside the last two furlongs Surplice and Canezou came right away from their rivals, and although neither the colt nor the filly flinched under pressure and Surplice was giving 5 pounds, he beat her by a neck in a driving finish with Flatcatcher 3 lengths away third. It was the first time that a Derby winner had won also the St. Leger since the year 1800.

As the winner was led in after the race, amidst the exultant hullabaloo which follows a Classic victory, Lord George was reminded again of his loss in selling his horses before they attained their greatest glory, although in his heart he was not certain that he grieved. He was a little tired of life and uncertain of his future. It was as though all the colour had been drained from his existence. He was a bachelor set in his habits, with many acquaintances and few close friends. He knew instinctively that he was unsuited in character for a long and brilliant Parliamentary career, and he knew, too, that he could never interest himself in the management of the Welbeck estates, for he was incapable of subjecting himself to the dictates of others. Goodwood, and its surrounding countryside was his love, but it would not be possible for him to make his home there permanently. In reality he was lonely, but too stubborn to radically alter his mode of life. Racing had lost its fascination for him, for there were so few new fields to conquer.

On the final day of the Doncaster meeting he watched Lord Stanley's Canezou brought out again to win the Park Hill Stakes and later in the afternoon walk-over for a sweepstake, and The Flying Dutchman add to his renown by a further spectacular victory, when he spread-eagled his field; he also saw Surplice given a walk-over. The final race of the day was a handicap won by a colt of Lord Clifden's in a close finish with one belonging to the Duke of Richmond. It was the last race that he ever saw, for six days later he was dead.

News of his death reached his cousin Charles Greville the following afternoon. For many years the two men had been estranged despite all attempts by their friends to heal their animosity. Yet Greville's entry in his diary is the most clear-sighted verdict on Bentinck.

'I have not the least doubt that, for his own reputation and celebrity, he died at the most opportune period. His fame had probably reached its zenith, and credit was given to him for greater abilities than he possessed, and for a futurity of fame, influence, and power which it is not probable he ever would have realized. As it is, the world will never know anything of those serious blemishes which could not fail to dim the lustre of his character. He will long be remembered and regretted as a very remarkable man, and will occupy a conspicuous place in the history of his own time.'

BIBLIOGRAPHY

T. H. BIRD. *Admiral Rous and the English Turf.* Putnam. 1939.

JOHN WILSON CROCKER. *The Crocker Papers* (3 vols.). London. 1884.

WILLIAM DAY. *Reminiscences of the Turf.* Richard Bentley & Son. 1886.

EARL OF BEACONSFIELD. *Lord George Bentinck. A Political Biography.* Longmans, Green & Co. 1881.

J. S. FLETCHER. *History of the St. Leger Stakes.* Hutchinson & Co. Ltd. 1927.

JOHN KENT. *Racing Life of Lord George Cavendish Bentinck.* William Blackwood & Sons. 1892.

JOHN KENT. *Reminiscences of Goodwood and the Dukes of Richmond.* Sampson Low, Marston & Co. 1896.

CHESTER KIRBY. *The English Country Gentleman.* James Clarke & Co. Ltd. 1937.

LORD WILLIAM LENNOX. *Memoirs of Charles Gordon Lennox, 5th Duke of Richmond.* Hurst. 1862.

LORD WILLIAM LENNOX. *Celebrities I have Known* (4 vols.). Hurst. 1876.

PHILIP MORRELL, Editor. *Leaves from the Greville Diarys.* Eveleigh Nash & Grayson. 1929.

ROGER MORTIMER. *The Jockey Club.* Cassell & Co. Ltd. 1958.

ROGER MORTIMER. *History of the Derby Stakes.* Cassell & Co. Ltd. 1962.

SQUIRE OSBALDESTON (E. D. Cuming, Editor). *Autobiography.* John Lane, The Bodley Head. 1926.

C. M. Prior. *History of the Racing Calendar*. Sporting Life, London. 1926.

A. S. Turberville. *A History of Welbeck Abbey and its Owners.* Faber & Faber Ltd. 1938 and 1939.

Whitewell Wilson, Editor. *The Greville Diary*. William Heinemann Ltd. 1927.

The Racing Calendar.   *The Sporting Life.*
Sporting Magazine   *The Times.*
The Morning Post

Index

165